MANAGING DIVERSITY FLASHPOINTS IN HIGHER EDUCATION

MANAGING DIVERSITY FLASHPOINTS IN HIGHER EDUCATION

Joseph E. Garcia and Karen J. Hoelscher

AMERICAN COUNCIL ON EDUCATION
PRAEGER
Series on Higher Education

Library of Congress Cataloging-in-Publication Data

Garcia, Joseph E.
  Managing diversity flashpoints in higher education / Joseph E. Garcia and Karen J. Hoelscher.
      p. cm. — (ACE/Praeger series on higher education)
    Includes bibliographical references and index.
    ISBN 978–0–275–98980–4 (alk. paper)
1. Education, Higher—United States. 2. Social learning—United States.
3. Socialization—United States. 4. Group identity—United States.
I. Hoelscher, Karen J. II. Title.
LA227.4.G37 2008
378′.017—dc22   2007038555

British Library Cataloguing in Publication Data is available.

Library of Congress Catalog Card Number: 2007038555
ISBN-13: 978–0–275–98980–4

First published in 2008

Praeger Publishers, 88 Post Road West, Westport, CT 06881
An imprint of Greenwood Publishing Group, Inc.
www.praeger.com

Printed in the United States of America

The paper used in this book complies with the
Permanent Paper Standard issued by the National
Information Standards Organization (Z39.48–1984).

10 9 8 7 6 5 4 3 2 1

CONTENTS

PREFACE

Our writing partnership grew out of a shared belief: faculty and staff can influence campus climate beyond teaching in a classroom or overseeing office tasks. Neither faculty nor staff tend to be trained in recognizing and responding to difficult interpersonal situations involving student-identity differences. To address these deficits, we wrote this book to share our research on how identity, privilege, and interpersonal skills impact the human spirit and our ability to learn, and to lay out specific steps that we can take to improve the learning environment.

The challenges of diversity in higher education affect us all. Even as definitions of diversity abound and the legacy of "isms" (e.g., racism, sexism, etc.) remain, questions of equity, fairness, and equality continue to be debated in society. At the same time, concerns about demographic changes, national and global security, global competitiveness, and social justice attract the attention of people around the globe.

Our work does not pretend to solve these larger societal questions. Rather, we take to heart the saying, think globally and act locally. We wrote this book to enable campus leaders to broaden their understanding of how small acts of courage create institutions where respect for individual identities encourages learning and educational achievement for all.

We offer a strategy for addressing difficult situations, which we label "diversity flashpoints," for faculty and staff, as well as institutional leaders. We acknowledge the importance of context as well as content in providing an approach that uses locally based data to reveal and address the flashpoints that most affect learning.

This book stems from the support of many people. We extend our appreciation to our interviewees, who shared the flashpoint incidents that you, your students, or a colleague may have experienced at your university. We thank our Western Washington University colleagues who encouraged us to move forward with the work: Sonia Arevalo-Hayes, David Brunnemer, Nancy Corbin, Patricia Fabiano, Ted Pratt, Peter Rosenberg, Michael Vendiola, and Carmen Werder. Thanks to Stan Wakefield, who matched us with Praeger-ACE, and to our editor Susan Slesinger, who has supported our work throughout. Thanks to our parents, Walt and Roberta Carlson and Eladio and Blanche Garcia, who provided the DNA and the nurturing that led us to a clear focus on improving interpersonal communication across differences. Finally, special appreciation goes to our mates, Chuck Hoelscher and Karen Copetas, for their infinite and loving support while we toiled away on this project.

We dedicate this book to future generations, including Elena and Tony Hoelscher, Emanuel and Angel Martinez, and Yamil, Carina, and Jeshua Linder.

CHAPTER

Introduction

Justice is conscience, not a personal conscience but the conscience of the whole of humanity. Those who clearly recognize the voice of their own conscience usually recognize also the voice of justice.
Alexander Solzhenitsyn, 1967 (Labedz, 1970)

When Solzhenitsyn spoke about justice, he had in mind the experience of life in a Gulag in Siberia. While the Gulag experience is far removed from the typical experience of university students, staff, and faculty in America, his comment on the voice of conscience holds true for all of us in our day-to-day interactions with others. In this book, we offer an informed strategy for being more thoughtful about how we express our voices of conscience to productively promote justice in higher education. We begin our discussion with a set of stories that turn out to be unusually common in higher education:

- A student angrily points out during one of your lectures that she is concerned about the coverage of typical developmental patterns of Native American preschoolers;

- Two staff members, in the presence of students speaking a language other than English, make a pointed comment that everyone should be speaking English on campus; and

- You overhear two students talking as you walk into class about someone "acting so gay" or referring to something as "so retarded."

This book is about addressing situations in higher education that faculty, administrators, staff, and students encounter—situations that threaten our collective sense of justice and community. These stories come from our own experience and represent a much larger set of experiences that occur frequently on campuses across the nation. The stories are about difficult situations that have the potential to spiral out of control and interfere with teaching, learning, and scholarship. They are not stories about intentionally racist or sexist people, but about collisions between individuals who experience and view the world in different ways. We call these stories *diversity flashpoint incidents,* which we formally define as difficult interpersonal situations that arise out of identity differences, and have the potential to become explosive.

Diversity flashpoint incidents are situations we encounter that have the potential to become destructive both to immediate participants and to bystanders. A diversity flashpoint incident results in the feeling that there has been a broken connection among those working together on the shared task of teaching and learning. Troubling to most is that the broken connection relates to membership in a group and brings up the presence of an "ism" (e.g., racism, sexism, etc.) that challenges open communication and learning. The way in which we address these difficult interpersonal situations can lead to outcomes that range from pain and suffering to more positive feelings of self-worth and enhanced learning.

Successfully managing a flashpoint situation requires knowledge, skill, and compassion. In addition to the challenges associated with difficult interpersonal situations among people who have common identities, situations where people have different social identities are both subtle and obvious in their complexity. The ability to anticipate, think about, and proactively manage such situations is a daunting task for many people, including professional educators. Many professionals in higher education have participated in some form of staff development for increasing sensitivity to or raising awareness of diversity issues. However, few of us have had the opportunity to develop skills that go beyond learning about others who are different, or being sensitive to the needs of people who are different from us. Acquiring such skills would enable us to behave in ways that are more mindful of the opportunities associated with difference.

In this chapter we offer a rationale for and an approach to developing skills for effectively managing difficult interpersonal incidents. We believe this approach can assist academic leaders in transforming their institutions into places where faculty and staff can become more effective in accomplishing their academic mission.

WHAT DO WE KNOW ABOUT DIVERSITY FLASHPOINTS?

The experience of having one's identity challenged is part of the everyday life of members of disenfranchised groups in America. Ellis Cose (1993), in his book on the experience of successful African Americans, poignantly illustrates this phenomenon. For example, he describes the experience of Ms. Lynn Walker, an African American woman and senior executive with the Ford Foundation, who one day, together with her white neighbors, was systematically picking through the garbage outside of their exclusive co-op apartments searching for the ownership of illegal construction debris that were dumped in the rubbish bins there. While the group was searching through the debris, a white homeless man happened upon the group. Cose writes, "He paused and then walked directly up to Walker and helpfully advised her that he had already scoured the rubbish and found nothing worthwhile. For a moment she was confused, but she suddenly realized that though she was dressed for work, the man had taken her for a fellow homeless person who was unemployed. Later she laughed over the bizarre episode but observed that it had driven home for her how pervasive a role racial assumptions can play" (p. 42). This story is of particular interest as it demonstrates that such an experience can happen to a successful and well-established professional living in an affluent neighborhood. One can only imagine how this situation might play out in the life of a college student.

Understanding the dynamics that underly events such as this one, as well as the stories mentioned at the beginning of this chapter, became a topic of interest to us during an assignment to conduct a diversity workshop for new faculty and their mentors in December 2000. For that session, we generated a set of vignettes from our own and our colleagues' experience that illustrated difficult situations faced by faculty around diversity.

The stories we used included:

- You find that you enjoy and are successful advising and giving support to students who are underrepresented in your department. As a result, you spend quite a bit of time with these students. One day in the workroom you overhear a colleague refer to you as "Dr. Diversity."

- A faculty member discovers that she is pregnant at the same time she is submitting her dossier for tenure and promotion. She wonders if she should tell her department chair or colleagues that she is pregnant.

- Last year your department interviewed a faculty candidate from a traditionally underrepresented group. Several faculty colleagues were uncomfortable with this person and treated the person in a cool and distant manner. Among other examples, only one person went to dinner with the candidate during the campus visit. This year, in another search by the department, one of your colleagues observes that the applicant pool has no candidates from this underrepresented group; you know from attending professional conferences that potential qualified candidates are available from this group. Another member of the department responds that you just can't get qualified candidates to apply because there are just so few of them and they get big-time jobs because of affirmative action.

The discussion of these vignettes at the faculty workshop was rich and lively. The participants connected with the flashpoint incident vignettes in terms of their own experiences and the experiences of their peers in higher education. We were impressed with the power of these vignettes as vehicles for stimulating conversation among our faculty colleagues and administrators in attendance. Reflecting on the use of this process led us to question the extent to which they were generalizable in terms of the experience of students, faculty, and staff on our campus and on other campuses in the United States. This prompted us to embark on a study of what we then labeled diversity flashpoints (Garcia, Hoelscher, and Farmer, 2005).

In our study we interviewed 34 student personnel administrators and faculty members from 11 colleges and universities in the United States. They worked in a wide range of universities, including large state universities, private undergraduate institutions, comprehensive public universities, and one historically black university.

The study taught us about the frequency of, characteristics of, relationships between, and consequences of diversity flashpoint incidents. Each of these areas will be described below.

First, for better or worse, diversity flashpoints are a normal part of university life, and are probably at play in most organizations. Our interviewees repeatedly impressed upon us that no matter where they worked, they had no difficulty generating stories that represented diversity flashpoint incidents. We were easily able to obtain 153 diversity flashpoint incidents that students had told them about or that they had personally observed.

Our second learning point resulted from classifying each of the incidents on the basis of their similarity. By doing this we discovered that the incidents could be organized in terms of the issue underlying the tension and the behavioral setting (i.e., context) in which the event occurred. This classification enabled us to better understand the

Table 1.1
Pattern of Incidents by Behavioral Settings and Issues

| Issues | Behavioral Settings | | | | |
	Expectations	Curriculum	Learning	Assessment	Total
Support Special Student	13	2	5	6	26
Treatment of a Lone Member of an Under-Represented Group	0	1	13	2	15
Treatment of Non-Native English Speakers	7	0	2	2	12
Interacting with Individuals who are Different	2	2	12	5	21
Use of Terms that Label Others in Ways that Devalue	6	4	19	6	35
Respond as an Ally	1	1	28	1	31
Recognizing and Valuing Others	0	2	8	0	10
Address the Use of Coercive Power	2	0	1	0	3
Total	31	12	88	22	153

underlying dynamics of these incidents (see Table 1.1). We were able to identify the following issues, which commonly contribute to the underlying tension inherent in flashpoint incidents:

- The need to explore and support special student needs for successful learning and growth,
- The ability to manage the treatment of a lone member of an underrepresented group so as to avoid treatment of the individual as representing all members of that group,
- The need to recognize the intelligence, knowledge, and perspectives of non-native English speakers,
- The ability to become more comfortable interacting with individuals who are different,
- The recognition that the use of terms that label others in ways that devalue and marginalize them through stereotypes or derogatory terms is inappropriate,
- The need to respond as an ally to individuals from traditionally underrepresented groups when they are made vulnerable to ridicule or marginalization,

- The importance of recognizing and valuing others and their perspectives, and
- The ability to recognize and address the use of coercive power to take direct advantage of others who are different.

In addition, our analysis generated the following four behavioral settings, the contexts in which these incidents occurred:

- Situations where expectations for learning are set and communicated,
- The learning content and nature of the curriculum,
- The interactive learning environment surrounding class discussions, advising, and student-to-student interaction, and
- The assessment process.

This classification exercise led to our third learning point: the occurrence of these incidents is not random. For example, we discovered that more than half of the incidents were associated with a limited number of settings and issues, thus offering the opportunity to use these categories as a heuristic tool for targeting efforts to address diversity flashpoint incidents. Specifically, we found that the majority of incidents occur in settings characterized by dynamic interactions involving faculty, students, and staff such as discussions in classroom settings or advising situations. The most pressing issues associated with these incidents were related to the use of terms that devalue and marginalize others (e.g., the use of the term "you people") and the need to respond as an ally (e.g., responding in a supportive manner after a student, faculty, or staff member makes a denigrating comment towards a member of a group that is different in some way).

Our final learning point involved recognizing the consequences of the pattern of diversity flashpoint incidents. Our interpretation suggests that, from a resource allocation perspective, faculty and staff development efforts in diversity should target the issues and settings that account for the preponderance of reported incidents. We also found that diversity flashpoint incidents associated with significant liability issues were represented in other categories but in more limited numbers. While incidents of this type were less evident, there may be more to the story. Certainly, issues such as the use of coercive power may be underreported or may occur less frequently than other, smaller insults; however, the use of coercive power may represent a more egregious event, such as sexual harassment in cases of sex for grades. So while our results may have taught us that the volume of certain categories of flashpoint incidents is large and should be a focus of attention, other less frequent but more serious, at least per incident, categories should not be ignored by administrative leadership and the general campus community. Furthermore, our results are an aggregate of stories from 11 institutions and this pattern may not be replicated within individual campuses. We will speak to this issue later in chapter 7, Going Local.

SKILL BUILDING FOR ADDRESSING DIVERSITY FLASHPOINTS

Since the 1980s, diversity training has become widely available and has developed many faces and objectives. Prominent among these are two types of effort: (1) attempts to develop empathy and sensitivity of majority individuals towards people who have been, and continue to be, the targets of systematic acts of injustice; and (2) attempts to increase cultural knowledge about people from these targeted groups. People who are sensitive to these issues can become more effective at helping to right historical and current wrongs. Efforts to enhance cultural knowledge assume that exposure to multicultural information increases understanding and tolerance. These efforts frequently take the form of sensitivity training aimed at putting participants in touch with the experience of oppression and injustice, or engaging people in cultural awareness and educational events such as Cinco de Mayo or Black History Month celebrations. We believe that awareness and sensitivity serve as a critical foundation in helping people to address issues of social injustice across identity groups. Being able to empathize and understand others and the factors that exist in creating inequity address our emotions and intellect and can provide a reason for, but may not ensure action.

In this book we address the gap between having reason for action and taking action. As a colleague of ours once said, "I have been to too many workshops where we learn to sing Kumbaya." His reaction to these experiences is revealing and points to the importance of providing well-meaning and informed individuals the skills to become more effective professionals. Through our engagement with faculty across the United States and on our campus we have found that working through diversity flashpoint incidents helps develop a real-time response informed by both an emotional connection to and an intellectual understanding of the issues.

Based on these experiences, we offer an action-based approach that provides the opportunity to develop a portfolio of skills directed at addressing issues embedded in real-life contexts. Described as the 4 R's approach in chapter 6, Understanding Diversity Flashpoint Situations, we activate what we have learned about the patterns of occurrence of flashpoint incidents, enabling professionals and others to:

- Recognize what is happening in a particular situation,
- Reflect on possible ways to address the incident,
- Respond in an informed manner, and
- Reassess the incident and the outcome of the intervention.

In the chapters that follow, we use principles from learning theory, competency building, and cross-cultural communication to inform the design of the curriculum for learning to address diversity flashpoints.

BUILDING A HEALTHY CLIMATE THROUGH DIALOGUE ABOUT FLASHPOINTS

Flashpoint incidents, when they occur, often take on the characteristics of the infamous "elephant in the living room." Everyone is aware of its existence, yet few are willing to accept and address the reality. Addressing the concern is uncomfortable, may involve dealing with defensiveness, managing loss of face, and confronting hurt and anger, all of which are conditions most people would rather avoid. Of course, sometimes an individual will speak out about such incidents, but his voice is likely to be ignored or discounted by responses such as, "Joe, you are just being too sensitive here," or, "That is an exceptional situation; the individual probably did something to warrant the response." Not unlike what happens to organizational whistle blowers, these individuals come to feel unwanted or even rejected ("Whistle-Blowers," 2002).

Our inability to engage in healthy dialogue forces us to ignore the elephant. In essence, talking about such incidents is nearly impossible because we personalize the event, placing blame on the individuals involved and stigmatizing them as racist, sexist, or politically incorrect. This halts conversation about the incident and the conditions that may have contributed to its occurrence.

Various efforts to promote dialogue are noteworthy. Notable in higher education is the work conducted at the University of Michigan in the Program on Intergroup Relations, an educational program that proactively promotes understanding of intergroup relations both inside and outside of the classroom through dialogue and discussion among students, faculty, and staff. Similar programs developed across the country have increased diversity awareness and understanding through focusing on student development (Schoem and Hurtado, 2001).

In this book we offer a professional development approach that guides faculty and staff to engage in dialogue and develop competencies to confront the elephants in the room so that we can all grow and become more healthy partners in learning. In our view, developing action-based competencies in diversity is critical to the success of higher education as the face of our nation changes and as the world becomes flat through the increasing global flow of people, goods, services, and education (Friedman, 2005).

PLAN OF THE BOOK

This book comprises three parts plus appendices. Part I examines the context of diversity. In Chapter 1, we offer a description of, a rationale for, and an approach to developing skills for effectively managing diversity flashpoint incidents. Chapter 2 focuses on diversity trends on university campuses. Chapter 3 outlines factors associated with a diversity-friendly college campus.

In Part II of the book we discuss the foundations necessary to develop skills for effectively addressing flashpoint incidents. In Chapter 4, we visit the topic of learning theory to provide a rationale for our approach to helping individuals become competent at learning to address a diversity flashpoint. In Chapter 5, we bring the reader's attention to basic communication and intercultural communication skills necessary for gracefully and successfully negotiating the flashpoint incident landscape.

Part III of the book introduces the reader to the 4 R's, an approach to addressing flashpoint incidents. Chapter 6 offers an inclusive strategy for informed action that is inclusive and provides for continuous learning and improvement in recognizing, reflecting on, and responding to flashpoint situations, and reassessing those responses. Chapter 7 discusses how to translate this general approach to the reader's specific campus or university environment. Chapter 8 introduces the reader to the challenges and resulting new opportunities for developing competencies in addressing diversity flashpoint incidents.

The book concludes with appendices that include a set of templates for working through the activities in the book, as well as a collection of diversity flashpoint incident vignettes representative of the findings from our research on college campuses in the United States. These vignettes serve as a window into the lives of students, faculty and staff, and administrators, illuminating the issues and contexts where these difficult situations occur, and act as a vehicle for applying the 4 R's strategy to address diversity flashpoint incidents.

REFERENCES

Cose, E. (1993). *The rage of a privileged class.* New York: HarperCollins Publishers.

Friedman, T. L. (2005). *The world is flat: A brief history of the twenty-first century.* New York: Farrar, Straus and Giroux.

Garcia, J. E., Hoelscher, K. J., & Farmer, V. L. (2005). Diversity flashpoints: Understanding difficult interpersonal situations grounded in identity difference. *Innovative Higher Education,* 29(4), 275–89.

Labedz, L. (Ed.). (1970). *Solzhenitsyn; a documentary record.* London: Allen Lane, Penguin Press.

Schoem, D., and Hurtado, S. (Eds.). (2001). *Intergroup dialogue: Deliberative democracy in school, college, community and workplace.* Ann Arbor: University of Michigan Press.

Whistle-Blowers Being Punished, A Survey Shows. (2002, September 3). *New York Times,* p. A14.

CHAPTER

Diversity Trends: Implications for Campuses

Change means movement. Movement means friction. Only in the frictionless vacuum of a nonexistent abstract world can movement or change occur without that abrasive friction of conflict.

Saul Alinsky (Alinsky, 1971)

DEMOGRAPHIC CHANGES

The United States has been and is a dynamic nation. Since its founding, immigrants have played a key role in shaping the political, economic, and demographic profile of the nation. Notwithstanding the forced immigration of Black Africans before the Civil War, prior to the middle of the twentieth century the majority of immigrants to the United States came from Europe. For example, some 18 million individuals entered the United States between 1890 and 1920. Most of these immigrants were Irish and German, followed by Italians and Eastern Europeans who were largely Catholic and Jewish (Booth, 1998).

However, since the beginning of the twentieth century fundamental shifts have occurred in the racial and ethnic population of the nation. In 1990, 1 in 8 Americans was of a race other than White; by 2000, this ratio shifted to 1 in 4 (Hobbs and Stoops, 2002). In contrast to early waves of immigrants, the majority of entrants into the United States since the 1970s have come from Asia and Latin America rather than Europe, bringing increasingly new cultures, intellectual viewpoints, and languages to the nation.

Following the Workforce 2000 report predicting these shifts in the U.S. population (Johnston and Packer, 1987), there has been increasing public awareness of the significance of these demographic changes. For example, nightly news reports feature immigration issues and census bureau reports, which indicates shifts in the majority and minority population trends (Immigration Daily News, 2007). Indeed, current U.S. Census figures confirm Johnston and Packer's predictions. In 1980, minorities made up 20.43 percent of the U.S. population; by 2000 that figure rose to 30.87 percent of the overall population. This trend continued into 2005 as 33 percent of the population was Hispanic and non-White (Social Science Data Analysis Network, n.d.).

In the context of these changes, the most dramatic demographic change has occurred among Hispanics, with an overall increase of 6.1 percent between 1980 and 2000 (Social Science Data Analysis Network, n.d.). In contrast to other immigrant groups, Hispanic immigrants tend to come from countries that are relatively near the United States where it is possible for individuals to maintain relationships with their country of origin. Furthermore, current forecasts indicate that by 2050 the non-Hispanic White population of the United States will have shrunk to a simple majority of just over 50 percent (The Project for Excellence in Journalism, 2004).

This will represent the lowest representation of non-Hispanic Whites in the history of the United States. The growth of the Hispanic population, the increase in the number of immigrants in the United States, and the slowing of the growth of the non-Hispanic White population signals a significant shift in the complexion of the U.S. population and its many institutions, including higher education.

MELTING POT OR MOSAIC

The melting pot metaphor was first applied to the American immigrant experience in 1908 in the play, "The Melting Pot," authored by Israel Zangwill, an English Jew and prolific author who advocated for a free Jewish state. This play advocated a path towards homogenizing all immigrants into a single unified American identity (Booth, 1998). While embraced by many, writers such as Horace Kallen (1915) contested this view by observing that the uniqueness of America is the diversity of peoples who had come to populate its shores and engage in a voluntary cooperative democracy. From Kallen's perspective, in America, people of each nationality expressed their own cultural and intellectual forms freely as engaged citizens. Kallen's view has subsequently been referred to as "the American mosaic" and aligns with notions of cultural pluralism. This is the belief that diversity and dissent are valuable to individuals and society.

The debate on the legitimacy of the melting pot and mosaic metaphors continues to thrive in America today. Federal and local legislative efforts to declare English as the official language and restrict immigration (e.g., Hulse, 2006) contrast with programs that encourage multiple views of diversity in corporations (e.g., Perez, 2005) and in institutions of higher education (e.g., Diversity Web, n.d.).

These divergent views of diversity serve as examples of an ongoing struggle between ideological positions. It is telling that the reality of the nation reflects patterns such as the continued vitality of urban ethnic enclaves across the nation combined with white flight to rural areas and small cities (Booth, 1998), which is hardly the sign of a melting pot. Where this ideological struggle will transport us as a nation is yet to be determined. Nonetheless, America continues to be a place where peoples from different cultural backgrounds and points of view come and live together. This mixture of peoples, however configured, will expand within the generations of new students in the K–20 school systems across the nation. Indeed, as the demographics of the American K–20 classroom evolve, so will our need, as educators, to respond effectively to the issues presented by our increasing diversity.

EQUALITY AND OPPORTUNITY

As in previous generations, new immigrants typically find it difficult to achieve high-wage jobs due to lack of local qualifications or recognition of qualifications acquired in their native country. This is particularly challenging for undocumented workers who come to the United States seeking relative prosperity. Perhaps more troublesome is the fact that as a group, many minorities, even after living in the United States for multiple generations, continue to be economically disadvantaged (Orrenius, 2004).

One indicator of economic health is home ownership, and minorities have not fared well on this factor. Hobbs and Stoops (2002) report that homeownership rates are lowest for minorities, with Hispanics having the lowest rates of home ownership at 45.7 percent in comparison to the non-Hispanic White ownership rate of 72.4 percent.

Another indicator of economic well-being is annual income. In their recent report, Bucks, Kennickell, and Moore (2006) show that although the median annual income level of minorities has risen from

$24,400 in 1995 to $29,800 in 2004, non-Hispanic Whites have also experienced a rise in median income. As a result, the disparity between non-Hispanic Whites and Hispanics and non-Whites has increased from $16,300 in 1995 to $19,600 in 2004.

While minorities are not the only group of people who experience economic challenges, as a group they represent a significant portion of a growing population that is becoming increasingly important to the creation of wealth and the quality of life in the United States. As such, it is incumbent upon educational institutions and its leaders to create opportunities for success that welcome members of these groups.

THE ROLE OF EDUCATION

In the early days of higher education in America, universities were typically private institutions that catered to the relative few who could afford tuition and living expenses. This landscape changed due to both technological change and the passage of the Morrill Acts of 1862 and 1890 (Goldin and Katz, 1999). Since the Morrill Acts, education, and in particular public higher education, has played a major role in providing access to opportunities for immigrants and for the ordinary citizen to become more successful in America. Likewise, the G.I. Bill opened the doors to hundreds of thousands of citizens, including the poor, without respect to race, religion, or ethnic background, for whom higher education would have been unreachable (Wilson, 1995).

Today, the promise of higher education is becoming more and more tenuous with tuition increases and reduced access to financial aid now the norm (Singletary, 2006). This trend, coupled with the relative disparity in the economic status of both immigrants and other minorities, has the potential to lead to a diminution of the reservoir of an educated population in the United States.

This becomes a more urgent problem as minority children swell the rolls of the American public school system. According to a 2002 U.S. Department of Education report entitled "The Condition of Education," in 1973 the percentage of minorities attending public schools was 23 percent. By 2000, 39 percent of the students in public school were non-White. We can expect this trend to continue as the median age of the Hispanic and non-White population in the United States is markedly lower than that of non-Hispanic Whites. This is because the birth rate for most minorities is higher than that for the non-Hispanic White population, and those immigrants to the United States tend to be relatively young. Given these factors and the economic status of minority populations, their ability to become successful in the context of higher education continues to be at risk.

HIGHER EDUCATION

As with public schools and the nation in general, university and community college demographic changes are already upon us. The report by Harvey and Anderson (2005) indicates that minority enrollment in higher education has risen across all ethnic and racial groups. They show, for example, that between 1991 and 2001 minority enrollment in higher education increased by 1.5 million, totaling 4.3 million students with Hispanics showing the greatest gains with a 75 percent increase. While the total enrollment of White students, 10.1 million, far exceeded minority student enrollment, White enrollment declined from a high of 10.6 million during the decade.

As minority participation in higher education has increased, so has female participation, creating a dramatic change in the gender balance of students in higher education. Hudson, Aquilino, and Kienzl (2005) reported that although male participation rates in higher education increased from 38 percent in 1974 to 41 percent in 2003, it was eclipsed by the growth in female participation rates from 33 percent to 51 percent over the same time period. Furthermore, the number of degrees obtained by women in fields traditionally populated by males has increased dramatically with significant shifts occurring in fields such as zoology, business administration, political science, law, and medicine (see Table 2.1).

Table 2.1
Percentage of Female Graduates in U.S. Higher Education Selected Fields 1971–72 and 1996–97

Field of Study	% Female Graduates 1971–72	% Female Graduates 1996–97
Zoology	22	50
Business Administration	10	49
Political Science	19	44
Law	7	44
Medicine	9	41

Source: Bellis, D., and W. Pfeiffer (2002). *Gender equity: Men's and women's participation in higher education*. Report to the Ranking Minority Member, Subcommittee on Criminal Justice, Drug Policy and Human Resources, Committee on Government Reform, House of Representatives, United States General Accounting Office: Washington, DC. Retrieved March 15, 2007 from http://www.gao.gov/new.items/d01128.pdf.

One can easily argue that the feminization of the college student population is an acknowledged reality. Taken together, the new set of demographics is changing the classroom and the workplace with more women
and minorities entering higher education than ever before and women
entering fields that have been traditionally male dominated.

IMPLICATIONS

In this section we describe how subtle, non-academic cultural barriers have alienating effects that negatively impact the prospects for
minority and female student and faculty success in higher education.
We also offer an alternative set of value assumptions for discussion that
would be more minority- and female-friendly in higher education.

As a group, the experience and expectations of minorities as they
enter higher education is different from majority White students. They
are more likely to be the first in their family to go to college, more
likely to have to rely on financial aid, and less likely to have contact
with professionals and individuals with experience in higher education.
They are also more likely to have experienced discrimination in some
form or been the target of racist or ethnic slurs. For visible minorities,
they also face being identified as different and treated in ways that are
a function of their physical appearance (e.g., skin color, hair texture)
that are uncomfortable or demeaning (Cose, 1993).

A history of these pejorative experiences is likely to make a person,
at the very least, cautious upon arrival on a college campus. Furthermore, hidden non-academic barriers impact minority student success
significantly more than non-Hispanic White students (Loo and Rolison, 1986). This research suggests that minority students, relative to
non-Hispanic White students, experienced greater pressure to accept
White middle-class values and, more importantly, reject their own values, reinforcing feelings of socio-cultural alienation.

As Loo and Rolison (1986) suggest, the image of the Ivory Tower
associates the privilege of higher education with non-Hispanic Whites.
A contrasting image might be that of an Ebony Tower leading to the
complementary question of how that might look in the eyes of non-
Hispanic White students. This critique does not intend to exclude or
discriminate against non-Hispanic Whites; rather, it encourages us to
reflect on our assumptions about how institutions of higher education
function in ways that are exclusionary in subtle but systematic and
powerful ways. In the classroom, laboratory, field projects, residence
halls, dining halls, student activities, and academic leadership venues

these assumptions serve as powerful lenses and determinants of what is and is not valued during everyday life on university campuses. If universities aim to provide quality education to all, then academic leadership must reassess the requisite knowledge, skills, and attitudes expected of and sup-ported among members of the university community.

As an approach to providing some relief from these alienating pres-sures, Loo and Rolison (1986) recommend, in addition to other initia-tives, increasing the number of minority faculty in academia. We agree that the presence of identifiable faculty and staff who share and respect the values and contributions of members of minority communities is one way to address this issue. However, even with successful efforts to alter the face of the academy, such as The PhD Project, which supports the recruitment and mentoring of minority doctoral students in the fields of business, the proportion of minority faculty and staff remains negligible in American universities. As Moreno, Smith, Clayton-Pedersen, Parker, and Teraguchi (2004) report, recent gains in the number of new minority faculty are mitigated by the poor retention rates of underrepresented minority faculty across the country. In terms of faculty, the socio-cultural alienation that students experience is a factor also associated with minority faculty turnover (Cora-Bramble, 2006; Trower and Chait, 2002).

Trower and Chait (2002) report a similar set of obstacles for women in academic settings, citing significant differences between the low number of female faculty members who reach full professor rank in doctoral granting institutions relative to the high number of female faculty who achieve full professor rank at colleges and universities lower in prestige. Again, cultural factors are implicated in contributing to this disparity.

In their analysis of the culture of the academy, Trower and Chait (2002) identified values that are largely ascribed to by minorities and women and are at odds with the traditional values of the academy. These include:

- Promotion and tenure review processes should be open and transparent;
- Merit is a socially constructed concept and can be renegotiated;
- Cooperation and collaboration are more desirable than competition;
- Problems (as opposed to disciplines) should drive research efforts;
- Teaching, advising, and service (as opposed to heavily weighting scholarship) should have a meaningful impact on faculty tenure and promotion decisions;

- Work–family balance is critical to developing and sustaining excellence among faculty;
- Faculty responsibilities are collectively as well as individually based.

As university responsibilities shift in response to changes in the makeup of the college student population and sustaining the diversification of faculty ranks, creating venues for having meaningful conversations in campus communities about values is a useful place to begin realigning efforts to act responsibly. It will be in these venues that Alinsky's ideas about movement and creative friction will come to fruition.

In Chapter 3 we review diversity climates on campus. As part of that review we explore the nature of climate and how to promote a diversity climate using examples from campuses across the United States. We also discuss how macro issues such as climate must serve as the foundation for everyday actions to achieve inclusion and equity on a university campus.

REFERENCES

Alinsky, S. (1971). *Rules for radicals: A practical primer for realistic radicals.* New York: Vintage Books.

Bellis, D., and W. Pfeiffer, W. (2000). *Gender equity: Men's and women's participation in higher education.* Report to the Ranking Minority Member, Subcommittee on Criminal Justice, Drug Policy and Human Resources, Committee on Government Reform, House of Representatives, United States General Accounting Office: WA, DC. Retrieved March 15, 2007, from http://www.gao.gov/new.items/d01128.pdf.

Booth, W. (1998, February 22). One Nation, Indivisible: Is It History? *The Washington Post*, p. A1.

Bucks, B. K., Kennickell, A. B., and Moore, K. B. (2006). Recent changes in U.S. family finances: Evidence from the 2001 and 2004 survey of consumer finances. *Federal Reserve Bulletin*, Retrieved February 1, 2007, from http://www.federalreserve.gov/pubs/bulletin/2006/financesurvey.pdf.

Cora-Bramble, S. (2006). Minority faculty recruitment, retention and advancement: Applications of a resilience-based theoretical framework. *Journal of Health Care for the Poor and Underserved*, 17(2), 251–5.

Cose, E. (1993). *The rage of a privileged class.* New York: HarperCollins Publishers.

Diversity Web (n.d.). Retrieved January 10, 2007, from http://www.diversityweb. org/diversity_innovations/institutional_leadership/index.cfm.

Goldin, C., and Katz, L. F. (1999). The shaping of higher education: The formative years in the United States, 1890 to 1940. *The Journal of Economic Perspectives*, 13(1), 37–62.

Harvey, W. B., and Anderson, E. L. (2005). *Minorities in higher education 2003–2004: Twenty-first annual status report (2005)*. Washington, DC: American Council on Education. Retrieved January 18, 2007, from http://www.acenet.edu/AM/Template.cfm?Section=Home&TEMPLATE=/CM/ContentDisplay.cfm&CONTENTID=3701.

Hobbs, F., and Stoops, N. (2002, November). *Demographic trends in the 20th century*, U.S. Census Bureau, Census 2000 Special Reports, Series CENSR-4, U.S. Government Printing Office, Washington, DC. Retrieved December 15, 2006, from http://www.jamesgoulding.com/Downloads/Census_Data_pdf/Population_Demographic_Trends_1900_2000_stats.pdf.

Hudson, L., Aquilino, S., and Kienzel, G. (2005). *Issue brief: Postsecondary participation rates by sex and race/ethnicity: 1974–2003*. Jessup, MD: U.S. Department of Education Institute of Education Sciences; NCES 2005-028.

Hulse, C. (2006, May 19). Senate votes to set english as national language. *New York Times*. Retrieved May 19, 2006, from http://www.nytimes.com/2006/05/19/washington/19immig.html?ex=1305691200&en=ba011a037f568a43&ei=5090&partner=rssuserland&emc=rss.

Immigration Daily News. (2007). Retrieved February 28, 2007, from http://www.idexer.com/.

Johnston, W. B., and Packer, A. (1987). *Workforce 2000: Work and workers for the twenty-first century*. Indianapolis, IN: Hudson Institute, Inc.

Kallen, H. M. (1915, February 25). Democracy versus the melting pot: A study of American nationality. *The Nation*.

Loo, C. M., and Rolison, G. (1986). Alienation of ethnic minority students at a predominantly white university. *The Journal of Higher Education*, 57(1), 58–77.

Moreno, J. F., Smith, D. G., Clayton-Pedersen, A. R., Parker, S., and Teraguchi, D. H. (2006). *The revolving door for underrepresented minority faculty in higher education: An analysis from the campus diversity initiative*. San Francisco, CA: The James Irvine Foundation. [Electronic Version] http://www.irvine.org/assets/pdf/pubs/education/insight_Revolving_Door.pdf.

Orrenius, P. (2004). *Immigrant assimilation: Is the U.S. still a melting pot?* Southwest Economy—Federal Reserve Bank of Dallas, 3, 1–5. [Electronic Version] http://www.dallasfed.org/research/swe/2004/swe0403a.pdf.

The PhD Project. (n.d.). Retrieved March 10, 2007, from http://www.phdproject.org/.

Perez, J. (2005, September). Diversity report: Top 40 companies. *Hispanic Business.com*. Retrieved October 25, 2006, from http://www.hispanicbusiness.com/news/newsbyid.asp?id=25161.

The Project for Excellence in Journalism (2004). *The population picture*. Retrieved January 20, 2007, from http://www.stateofthemedia.org/2005/narrative_ethnicalternative_poppicture.asp?media=9.

Singletary, M. (2006, November 4). Loans only pay so much at college. *Seattle Post-Intelligencer.* [Electronic version] Retrieved November 15, 2006, from http://seattlepi.nwsource.com/money/291099_singletary04.html.

Social Science Data Analysis Network. (n.d.). *Census Scope.* Retrieved January 10, 2007, from http://www.censusscope.org/us/chart_race.html.

Trower, C. A., and Chait, R. P. (2002). Faculty diversity: Too little for too long. *Harvard Magazine,* 104(4), 33–37.

U.S. Department of Education, National Center for Education Statistics. (2002). *The Condition of Education 2002.* NCES 2002–025, Washington, DC: U.S. Government Printing Office.

Wilson, R. (1995, Fall). The G.I. Bill and the transformation of America. *National Forum.* Retrieved December 10, 2006, from http://www.find articles.com/p/articles/mi_qa3651/is_199510/ai_n8720508.

CHAPTER 3

Diversity-Friendly Campus Climates

Every community is an association of some kind and every community is established with a view to some good; for everyone always acts in order to obtain that which they think good.

Aristotle, 384–323 B.C. (Barnes, 1985)

COMMUNITY AND THE COLLECTIVE GOOD

Aristotle's notion about the nature of community remains relevant to life in modern organizations, especially in institutions of higher education. The good of higher education in America today is in the advancing of opportunities for students, contributing to the development of knowledge and understanding, and making society a better place to live (Freeland, 2004). How leaders in higher education act in alignment with these attributes varies by institution. Every university constitutes a unique community and, as Aristotle's quote asserts, attempts to achieve a collective good.

In this chapter, we illustrate how the context that surrounds individual action influences the determination of the collective good of diversity. We open with a discussion of context and diversity climate, and then offer examples of universities that have engaged in efforts to enhance their campus diversity climate. We close with some thoughts about the importance of the role of diversity climate in enabling individuals to engage in conversations about moving past the interpersonal missteps that occur in everyday life in higher education because of identity difference.

CONTEXT FOR BEHAVIOR

As the English poet John Donne (1627/1996) so eloquently noted, "no man is an island," and every organization provides a context in which human interaction and interconnectedness occurs. This context provides the physical and socio-psychological setting in which we operate. The physical elements of the setting (e.g., sound, lighting, temperature, cleanliness, amount of clutter) set boundaries around the shared expectations people have about the physical reality of everyday life. For example, relative to quieter environments, people in noisy environments are less likely to talk with each other, or if they do they will shout.

In contrast, the socio-psychological context tends to be more nuanced but has effects that are just as far reaching. When we consider the socio-psychological context of an organization, we must reflect on the discussion of organizational climate and culture. Dennison (1996) notes that researchers continually debate the exact meaning of these two terms, climate and culture, which are complex and intertwined. However, for our purposes we will use the term *climate* as the construct for helping us understand how the socio-psychological context impacts behavior and, more specifically, interaction associated with differences. We therefore accept the perspective that organizational climate mirrors the shared perceived expectations, norms, and conventions for behavior in an organization (Reichers and Schneider, 1990). While not unrelated, the term *culture* has been associated with deeper and more enduring aspects of the values and relationships that exist in an organization (e.g., core values, assumptions, rituals).

Organizational climate research demonstrates that climates differ on a range of attributes such as innovation (e.g., Klein and Sorra, 1996), creativity (e.g., Mumford, Scott, Gaddis, and Strange, 2002), and warmth and support (e.g., Field and Abelson, 1982). Since Hall and Sandler's article (1982) citing the chilly classroom climate for women, diversity has become recognized as a legitimate attribute of organizational climate. More recently, Hurtado, Milem, Clayton-Pedersen, and Allen (1998) demonstrated that numerous perceptions contribute to the racial climate of an institution, including the perceptions of exclusion from an institution's cultural traditions, the quality and frequency of cross-race interactions, the representation of racial groups in curriculum content, and, finally, the physical presence of members of racial and ethnic groups. These shared perceptions contribute to a climate of diversity, racial and beyond, that influences behavior of the members of the greater campus community.

Shared perceptions about diversity are likely to have a greater impact on our experience than physical setting. However, it is important to acknowledge an obvious exception to this assertion—physical abilities and challenging physical environments. For example, a campus without accessible entryways speaks loudly to the lack of appreciation and respect for differences in physical ability, as do libraries without desktop magnifiers for the visually impaired and college courses with limited numbers of signers for the hearing impaired. While campus accessibility, resources, or the availability of assistance devices have powerful impacts, these types of factors are relatively easy to identify, and, with sufficient resources, address.

In contrast, the impact of diversity and inclusiveness is both ubiquitous and momentary as manifest by the shared interactions of individuals in a community. Nonetheless, research shows that diversity climate influences a number of important dimensions of organizational life. These include how individuals feel about their life in the organization (e.g., their commitment, satisfaction, intent to stay or leave) and how they perform (Cox, 1993). For example, in a study of retail managers (Hicks-Clarke and Iles, 2000) diversity climate was defined in terms of policy support, organizational justice, and a welcoming attitude towards diversity was associated with positive organizational attitudes. Furthermore and more directly related to challenges in higher education, inhospitable campus climates are associated with increased drop-out rates for Latino, African American, and Native American students (McClellan, Cogdal, Lease, and Londono-McConnell, 1996; Loo and Rolison, 1986; Ponterotto, 1990).

CHARACTERISTICS OF DIVERSITY CLIMATE

Four divergent themes are widely acknowledged when defining diversity climate (Cox, 1993; Hughes et al., 1998; Hyde and Hopkins, 2004; Mayhew, Grunwald, and Dey, 2005; Mor Barak, Cherin, and Berkman, 1998; Szalacha, 2003). These include (see Table 3.1):

- Perceptions of degree of between-group conflict and acceptance of others,
- Level of institutional commitment to diversity (e.g., promotion of personal and emotional safety, promotion of increased demographic representation of individuals from minority populations),
- Fairness (e.g. acculturation processes, lack of institutional bias), and
- A generalized atmosphere of respect (e.g., personal attitudes and reduction of prejudices).

Table 3.1
Characteristics of Diversity Climate

Author	Diversity Climate Factors
Cox, T. (1993)	• Individual factors (personal identity structures, prejudice, stereotyping, personality type) • Intergroup factors (cultural differences, ethnocentrism, intergroup conflict) • Organizational factors (culture, acculturation processes, structural integration, institutional bias)
Hughes, M., Anderson, R., Cannon, J. H., Perez, E., and Moore, H. A. (1998)	• Perceived friendliness, safety, and acceptance across diverse groups
Hurtado, S., Milem, J. F., Clayton-Pederson, A., and Allen, W. A. (1998)	• Historical legacy of inclusion or exclusion of various racial or ethnic groups • Structural diversity (the numerical and proportional representation of diverse groups on campus) • Psychological climate (perceptions, attitudes, and beliefs about diversity) • Behavioral climate (how different racial and ethnic groups interact on campus)
Hyde, C. A., and Hopkins, K. (2004)	• Degree of member heterogeneity • Efforts to promote and sustain an environment conducive to maximizing the benefits of that heterogeneity
Mayhew, M. J., Grunwald, H. E., and Dey, E. L. (2005)	• Overall views about campus diversity • Perception of institutional commitment to diversity • Current interaction with diverse peers • Perceptions of interactions with diverse faculty • Student involvement with on-campus activities • Participation in diversity-related course learning • Perceptions of curricular diversity • Student demographics • Pre-college interactions with diverse peers
Mor Barak, M. E., Cherin, D. A., and Berkman, S. (1998)	• Organizational factors (fairness, inclusion) • Personal factors (diversity value, personal comfort)
Szalacha, L. A. (2003)	• Perceived level of safety • Tolerance and atmosphere of respect for sexual minority individuals

Themes less often mentioned by researchers include diversity in the curriculum, interaction with diverse faculty members, and factors related to personality characteristics of others. While this portrait of diversity climate is limited to these seven studies, it is telling that curriculum and opportunities to interact with diverse faculty members were infrequently mentioned as elements of diversity climate. These authors seem to agree that conditions that impact everyday life such as safety, feeling included, and clear messages supporting diversity made by leadership in the institution are the key elements of diversity climate.

Together, these studies provide information that can inform institutional policy on cultivating a positive diversity climate. As we describe in the next section, numerous colleges and universities are already investing in developing diversity-friendly campus initiatives.

ENHANCING DIVERSITY CLIMATE

In this section we describe research-based prescriptions for improving diversity climate. After that discussion we highlight a number of recognized approaches, with an emphasis on specific initiatives that have gained widespread acceptance as vehicles for advancing positive diversity climates.

Today, many universities are committed, in principle, to improving diversity climate. A casual review of reports of diversity practices in higher education by the American Association of College and Universities (AAC&U, n.d.) yields a substantial listing of university initiatives to enhance the climate for diversity and the academic success of minority faculty and students (AAC&U).

Diversity climate, which is a relatively abstract phenomenon resulting from community interactions, requires more than a unidimensional strategy for improvement. Enhancing the diversity climate on campus requires a comprehensive approach. Indeed, attempts to enhance organizational diversity through structural change (e.g., increasing and broadening an organization's demographic profile) have been judged inadequate without efforts to alter group norms and climate (Kossek, Markel, and McHugh, 2003). This finding is corroborated by the work of Gurin, Dey, Hurtado, and Gurin (2002), who demonstrated that although human ethnic and racial diversity is a necessary condition for climate change, it is the active engagement among the diversity of people on campus that is the key to fostering student learning and development.

In other words, there is no simple or quick fix. For example, Cox's well-known model for managing organizational change and enhancing diversity (1993; 2001) requires as essential the components of organizational leadership, research and measurement, education, the alignment of management systems, and follow-up. Although examples of recognized efforts to enhance diversity climate and change in institutions of higher education may not fully reflect Cox's model, they all share the philosophy that a multi-faceted approach is essential to produce tangible success.

Specifically, Milem, Chang, and Antonio (2005) argue that leadership efforts to develop a positive campus racial climate must attend to a core set of campus policies and practices. These include:

- Reconciling institutional history,
- Affirming diversity as policy,
- Monitoring and dispelling myths about campus balkanization,
- Creating safe cultural spaces,
- Transforming classroom environments, including having a diverse faculty,
- Using inclusive pedagogy and content, integrating diversity into student learning goals, and
- Maximizing opportunities for effective intergroup interaction and appreciation.

It is worth noting that Milem et al.'s (2005) list of leadership actions require ongoing efforts typical of improvements associated with process (as opposed to finite) outcomes. This suggests that diversity climate is always a work in progress and not work that can be initiated and forgotten. In the next section we offer examples of four universities with comprehensive plans for improving diversity climate, systems worthy of replication (AAC&U, n.d.).

A SAMPLE OF UNIVERSITY EXPERIENCES

Today, most universities have attempted to weave aspects of diversity into the fabric of the institution. Examples of institutional investment in diversity can be found in the form of equal opportunity–based legal compliance through human resource departments or via ethnic student support services, academic and co-curricular programming, or faculty development efforts. Certainly the form in which diversity is supported varies widely by institution.

In the following paragraphs we summarize the approaches of four universities, all recognized by the AAC&U as having invested significantly in diversity and in improving diversity climate. These universities serve as useful benchmarks of current practice and are not meant to be representative of any systematic rating of schools on a measure of diversity effectiveness. In addition to having been recognized, we selected these four schools on the basis of geographic diversity in the United States. The four schools are Rutgers University, Central Michigan University, Kennesaw State University, and San José State University.

Rutgers University

Rutgers University, the major doctoral-granting state university in New Jersey, has made an institution-wide commitment to enhance a "climate of respect for diversity by fostering academic and public service multidisciplinary collaborations that advance intercultural and intergroup relations across ethnic, racial, class, trans-gender boundaries, and across disciplines" (Rutgers University Website, Office of Intercultural Activities, n.d.). Accordingly, the Rutgers University Office of Intercultural Initiatives is committed to:

- Enhancing intergroup relations among the various constituencies in the Rutgers community,
- Disseminating knowledge about intercultural relations in collaboration with other units on campus,
- Advancing social pluralism at Rutgers through partnerships in the university and in the external community, and
- Increasing connections with mainstream organizations on issues related to globalization and cross-cultural understanding.

A goal of promoting diversity and inclusion is included in the university's mission statement as well as in extensive academic programs and university-wide support for increasing knowledge about intercultural relations. Notable at Rutgers is their effort, funded by Bildner Family Foundation, to enhance intercultural interaction among members of the Rutgers community. This effort includes curricular and co-curricular offerings to promote skills in intercultural competence, a faculty multicultural fellows program, and the ethnic oral history performance project engaging students in learning and appreciating diversity through research in ethnic communities.

Central Michigan University

Central Michigan University, through their Office of Institutional Diversity, states that "diversity requires increasing the number of under-represented faculty, staff and students and fostering an educational community that values, respects, reflects and retains diversity" (Central Michigan University Website, *Office for Institutional Diversity*, n.d.). Like Rutgers, diversity climate is identified by reference to the qualities of the campus community and is an important aspect of their university's strategic plan.

Central Michigan University is a doctoral-granting public university with an enrollment of over 20,000 students. Unlike Rutgers, the leading doctoral university in the New Jersey, Central Michigan University is one of several public universities that are doctoral-granting universities in Michigan. At Central Michigan University, there is an institutional commitment to creating a positive climate for diversity, including a formal commitment by the university president that supports an antidiscrimination policy and other efforts to create an environment of respect for all.

In addition to the president's verbal support, there are a number of resources on campus that promote awareness and skill-building in intercultural understanding and dealing with difference. These range from programs and events that foster intergroup understanding to offices that provide services to enhance academic, personal, and professional student success for minority populations. More significant, in our view, is the development of a university strategic plan for diversity that is well articulated and is connected to university action. The goals cited in the plan are (Central Michigan University Website, *Strategic Plan*, n.d.):

- Create a community that values diversity,
- Recruit and support the administrative and organizational structure needed to coordinate and monitor diversity climate,
- Recruit, hire, retain, and promote faculty and staff who will enhance diversity across all levels and areas of the university,
- Recruit and retain students from a diversity of backgrounds, especially those from underrepresented groups,
- Provide professional development activities that assist all personnel in the understanding of their own and other cultures, and
- Infuse diversity into the curriculum and promote pedagogical strategies that encourage student involvement and facilitate respect of diverse perspectives.

It is worth noting that creating and supporting a diversity-positive climate are the leading goals in the plan. The plan includes specific and measurable objectives such as including diversity as an element in unit-performance evaluations, including considerations of diversity in the development of the physical environment, and in making decisions on the selection and placement of artwork. To reach these goals, the university supports training for new and continuing faculty and staff on diversity issues and for development of effective ways of managing interpersonal issues that have diversity implications.

Kennesaw State University

Kennesaw State University, located in suburban Atlanta, Georgia, is a public university of nearly 20,000 students with significant undergraduate and graduate programs. This university has also taken steps to incorporate diversity initiatives that recognize the importance of fostering a positive diversity climate. Kennesaw State University is currently implementing a formal diversity strategy through their Division of Legal Affairs and Diversity (Kennesaw State University Website, *Division of Legal Affairs and Diversity*, n.d.). In addition to implementing this strategy, the division handles the university's legal affairs, equal employment and opportunity, and university and community educational programs and events to foster diversity awareness.

As part of the university's strategic plan for diversity, Kennesaw State University has identified a set of challenges that fit within a framework for enhancing diversity efforts as they evolve in units across the campus. The framework recognizes four dimensions:

- Increasing the numbers of underrepresented populations at the university,
- Enhancing both climate and intergroup relations,
- Developing relevant competencies for a diverse world, and
- Supporting sustainable leadership to achieve the plan's goals.

In addition to these efforts, the university has programs that offer students information about cultures and groups that represent society, both locally and globally, directed at improving the campus diversity climate.

San Jose State University

San José State University, with over 30,000 students, is a master's-granting public university located in the heart of Silicon Valley in California. In the mid-1990s the campus embarked on a series of self-examinations on campus climate. From those studies, San José State developed a set of formal initiatives that feature a commitment to developing a climate that values diversity (San Jose State University Website, *Diversity and Campus Climate*, n.d.). These initiatives are part of their Western Association of School and Colleges accreditation report as formal policy. In addition to formal policy, the university provides active diversity support in many ways, including academic programming, employee resources from the office of equal opportunity for addressing issues of discrimination and diversity awareness, and student resources from the MOSAIC Cross-Cultural Center.

THEMES AND PRACTICES

In terms of promoting a diversity-positive climate, these four universities share the following important practices. First, academic leadership has made both real and symbolic statements about the importance of promoting the creation and maintenance of a welcoming atmosphere to people from different places into the life of the university. These statements can be found in the university's mission, strategic plan, or policies approved by the campus community. The statements are public pronouncements against which senior leadership makes both a personal claim and establishes the reputation of the institution.

Second, these statements are typically linked to the allocation of resources to achieve diversity and diversity climate–related goals. In several cases, these goals are tied to increasing the participation of members of underrepresented groups in the institution. More often, the actions support efforts to raise awareness, build competencies in working with others, and appreciate differences. Less frequently, we find institutions making specific statements linked to individual and/or unit performance evaluations and diversity.

It is fair to say that the recommendations of Milem, Chang, and Antonio's (2005) are in large part incorporated into the practices of these four universities. One might argue about how well they are articulated and to what extent the individual recommendations fit into the context of each of these schools. In addition, it is not always clear how these efforts are linked to performance metrics against which progress toward meeting these goals are measured or supported. However, on balance, the notion that creating a diversity-positive climate is multidimensional is affirmed by the approaches used by these schools. One generalized lesson that surfaces as true is worth noting: creating a climate that promotes diversity is an ongoing proposition and demands continuing attention, resources, review, and renewal.

In chapter four, we examine approaches to learning that support skill development and build institutional capacity.

REFERENCES

American Association of Colleges and Universities (AAC&U). (n.d.) Retrieved March 1, 2007, from http://www.aacu.org/issues/diversity/index.cfm.

Aristotle (384–323 B.C.), Politics 1.1.; 1252a1-6 (1985). In J. Barnes (Ed.), *The complete works of Aristotle*. Princeton: Princeton University Press.

Central Michigan University: Office for Institutional Diversity. (n.d.). *Strategic plan*. Retrieved March 1, 2007, from http://www.diversity.cmich.edu/strategicplan2.htm.

Cox, T. (1993). *Cultural diversity in organizations: Theory, research and practice*. San Francisco: Berrett-Koehler.

Cox, T. (2001). *Creating the multicultural organization*. San Francisco: Jossey-Bass.

Dennison, D. R. (1996). What is the difference between organizational culture and organizational climate? A native's point of view on a decade of paradigm wars. *Academy of Management Review*, 21(3), 619–54.

Donne, J. (1627/1996) Meditation XVII. In R. Andrews, M. Biggs, and M. Seidel (Eds.), *The Columbia world of quotations*. New York: Columbia University Press/Harmondsworth, Penguin.

Field, R. H. G., and Abelson, M. A. (1982). Climate: A reconceptualization and proposed model. *Human Relations*, 35(3), 181–201.

Freeland, R. M. (2004). Strengthening the foundation of a democratic society. *Presidency*, 7(3), 24–7.

Gurin, P., Dey, E.L., Hurtado, S., and Gurin, G. (2002). Diversity and higher education: Theory and impact on educational outcomes. *Harvard Educational Review*, 72(3), 330–66.

Hall, R. M., and Sandler, B. R. (1982). *The classroom climate: A chilly one for women? Project on the status and education of women*. Washington, DC: Association of American Colleges.

Hicks-Clarke, D., and Iles, P. (2000). Climate for diversity and its effects on career and organisational attitudes and perceptions. *Personnel Review*, 29(3), 324–46.

Hughes, M., Anderson, R., Cannon, J. H., Perez, E., and Moore, H. A. (1998). Campus racial climate policies: The view from the bottom up. *Race, Gender & Class*, 5(2), 139–57.

Hurtado, S., Milem, J. F., Clayton-Pederson, A., and Allen, W. A. (1998). Enhancing campus climates for racial/ethnic diversity: Educational policy and practice. *Review of Higher Education*, 21(3), 279–302.

Hyde, C. A., and Hopkins, K. (2004). Diversity climates in human service agencies: An exploratory assessment. *Journal of Ethnic & Cultural Diversity in Social Work*, 13(2), 25–43.

Kennesaw State University. *Division of legal affairs and diversity.* (n.d.). Retrieved March 1, 2007, from http://www.kennesaw.edu/diversity/

Klein, K. J., and Sorra, J.S. (1996). The challenge of innovation management. *Academy of Management Review,* 21(4), 1055–80.

Kossek, E. E., Markel, K. S., and McHugh, P. P. (2003). Increasing diversity as an HRM change strategy. *Journal of Organizational Change Management,* 16(3), 328–52.

Loo, C. M., and Rolison, G. (1986). Alienation of ethnic minority students at a predominantly white university. *The Journal of Higher Education,* 57(1), 58–77.

Mayhew, M. J., Grunwald, H. E., and Dey, E. L. (2005). Curriculum matters: Creating a positive climate for diversity from the student perspective. *Research in Higher Education,* 46(4), 389–412.

McClellan, S. A., Cogdal, P. A., Lease, S. H., and Londono-McConnell, A. (1996). Development of the multicultural assessment of campus programming (MAC-P) questionnaire. *Measurement and Evaluation in Counseling and Development,* 29(2), 86–99.

Milem, J. F., Chang, M. J., and Antonio, A. L. (2005). *Making diversity work on campus: A research-based perspective.* Washington, DC: Association of American Colleges and Universities.

Mor Barak, M. E, Cherin, D. A., and Berkman, S. (1998). Organizational and personal dimensions in diversity climate. *The Journal of Applied Behavioral Science.* 34, 82–104.

Mumford, M. D., Scott, G., Gaddis, B., and Strange, J. M. (2002). Leading creative people: Orchestrating expertise and relationships. *Leadership Quarterly,* 13(5), 705–50.

Ponterotto, J. G. (1990). Racial/ethnic minority and women students in higher education: A status report. *New Directions for Student Services,* 52, 45–59.

Reichers, A. E., and Schneider, B. (1990). Climate and culture: An evolution of constructs. In B. Schneider (Ed.), *Organizational climate and culture.* San Francisco: Jossey-Bass.

Rutgers University. *Office of Intercultural Activities.* (n.d.). Retrieved March 1, 2007, from http://intercultural.rutgers.edu/index.htm.

San Jose State University. *Diversity and Campus Climate.* (n.d.). Retrieved March 1, 2007, from http://www.sjsu.edu/wasc/portfolio/Metro_University/diversity/.

Szalacha, L. A. (2003). Safer sexual diversity climates: Lessons learned from an evaluation of Massachusetts safe school program for gay and lesbian students. *American Journal of Education,* 110(1), 58–88.

CHAPTER

Learning

By three methods we may learn wisdom: First, by reflection, which is noblest; second, by imitation, which is easiest; and third by experience, which is the bitterest.

Confucius, Chinese philosopher & reformer, 551–479 B.C.
(Quoteland.com, n.d.)

LEARNING AND WISDOM

The road to developing effective relationships requires learning and wisdom. As Confucius noted, we can achieve wisdom in many ways; experiencing the world of hard knocks is the most costly. In this chapter, we begin with the assumption that enabling individuals to meet the challenge of diversity flashpoint incidents is teachable. We believe the necessary skill set is scaffolded by understanding how people effectively address difficult interpersonal situations. By "effectively" we mean addressing the situation so the difficulty is bridged in a manner that acknowledges both differences and common goals and avoids creating interpersonal pain and distrust for those involved.

In the following sections, we explore models of learning beginning with a review of the role of theories of learning as frameworks for later chapters aimed at skill development. Next we discuss how learning how to learn makes us better learners and enables us to progress wisely toward addressing diversity flashpoint situations. Finally, we introduce the concept of organizational learning as a way of focusing our thinking toward building institutional capacity.

LEARNING BASICS

Psychologists and educators have invested enormous effort in the study of learning. This effort has spawned a wide range of theories and approaches to understanding learning including, but not limited to, behavioral (e.g., Skinner, 1950), cognitive (e.g., Miller, Galanter, and Pribram, 1960), experiential (e.g., Rogers and Freiberg, 1994), social learning (Bandura, 1977), and self-efficacy (Bandura, 1997) interpretations. While significant differences exist among these approaches, there are commonalities. We use the following definition of learning as it takes into consideration these various approaches. Learning is a "relatively permanent change, due to experience, either in behavior or in mental representations or associations" (Ormrod, 2006).

LEARNING AND OVERT BEHAVIOR

Behavioral theories of learning emphasize the importance of a change in response as *prima facie* evidence of the occurrence of learning (e.g., Skinner, 1950). Learning, according to behaviorists, is determined by the relationship between a stimulus and a response. When presented with a stimulus that has reinforcing attributes, behavior that precedes the stimulus is strengthened and is demonstrated more frequently and with greater strength. Concepts such as feedback, reinforcement, and reward are central to behavioral approaches to learning as they provide the underpinnings of behavioral change. For example, faculty members are more likely to use a teaching technique if students respond with interest and enthusiasm as a result of the use of the technique.

These principles underlie behavior modification programs. Behavior modification has been used in a wide range of organizational settings to change behavior by training people to perform specific technical tasks as well as work more effectively with others (Babb and Kopp, 1978). While many organizational behavior modification programs have generated positive results, behavior modification has been criticized on several grounds. Prominent among the criticisms is that learning is conceptualized and understood entirely from the relationship between external factors that oversimplify the learning process, ignoring the role of internal processes such as awareness and understanding (Babb and Kopp, 1978; Kreitner and Luthans, 1984). In the next section, we consider how processes that lie beneath observable behavior are tied to learning.

COVERT PROCESSES IN LEARNING

While we do not argue with the notion that actions speak loudly, we acknowledge, as many learning theorists note, that significant learning processes are covert. By "covert" we mean internal affective and cognitive processes that are not directly observable, but can be inferred and can influence learning. For example, motivation is an important covert process in the learning equation. Early learning theorists, such as Hull (1943), recognized the importance of an individual's drive or need as a basis for learning to occur. Without such a need, the learner is less attentive and less willing to practice. According to Hull, gaining knowledge is satisfying to the extent that the learning satisfies the desire to know or learn. Others, such as Rogers and Freiberg (1994), have placed motivation to learn as central to the learning processes. In addition, they advance the notion that learning that is perceived to be threatening to self is avoided; so for learning to occur, threat to self must be low. Together, these scholars argue that motivation fuels the learner's intentions to acquire knowledge and skills.

Miller (1956) demonstrated that learning and memory could be represented as an information processing function. For example, he found that attention span is limited to seven plus or minus two bits of information, and that human cognitive processes are regulated by this limit. Moreover, this finding supports the view that learning is governed by cognitive processes, such as short-term memory functioning, that are covert and not directly observable (Miller, Galanter, and Pribram, 1960). Next, we examine social learning theory.

SOCIAL LEARNING

Bandura (1977) introduced the idea that learning can occur through mere observation and does not require the production of a response. Accordingly, learning is a social phenomenon where observed behavior and its consequences serve as a model for action and is rehearsed symbolically prior to enacting the behavior overtly (Baldwin, 1992; Latham and Sari, 1979). For example, many faculty teach using a style adapted from observing a favorite teacher or set of teachers they experienced as students.

Social learning theory acknowledges that, in addition to behavior, the individual learner is engaged in covert, cognitive, and motivational processes. Motivation is in part derived through observing the positive and negative outcomes of other people's behavior. This is born out by results of experiments that indicate individuals are more likely to engage in an observed behavior if the individual model is more like themselves, is attractive, and if the outcome of the model's behavior is valued (Bandura, 1986; Goldstein and Sorcher, 1975).

From a social learning perspective, the power of social models cannot be underestimated. In addition to learning specific behaviors from watching others, individuals learn to recognize the context in which the behavior occurs and the consequences associated with the behavior. Furthermore, when individuals observe behaviors that are followed by positive outcomes, these behaviors are more rapidly incorporated into the learner's knowledge base, as they become the object of reproduction through mental rehearsal. We turn next to the concept of self-efficacy, which links feelings of confidence to effective learning and performance.

Self-Efficacy

Extending social learning theory, Bandura (1986; 1997) developed the concept of self-efficacy to explain how the beliefs individuals hold about their capability to act in ways that will influence the world around them in meaningful ways affect learning, motivation, and performance. Individuals with high levels of self-efficacy feel confident about investing time and energy to address challenging tasks. Strong self-efficacy results from successfully achieving goals in the face of adversity, gaining exposure to successful models familiar to the learner, and receiving encouragement and support from others.

According to Bandura (as cited in Combs and Luthans, 2007), developing self-efficacy requires that an individual experience enactive mastery, role modeling, positive persuasion, and emotional arousal. Enactive mastery can be achieved through discussing case scenarios and/or engaging in role-playing to build feelings of competence. Role modeling requires demonstrations (either live or recorded) of individuals performing required behaviors in a meaningful context that presents the consequences of the model's attitudes and behavior. Positive persuasion relies on the framing of the conversation by a facilitator who encourages learners to develop confidence in their ability to perform the new behaviors. Facilitators also serve in a motivational role. They provide both emotional support for learners to address the challenges of developing competencies and assist in developing emotional arousal or enthusiasm to learn by reinforcing the relevance, purpose, and value of the learning.

Multiple Perspectives on Learning and Learning to Learn

Learning to address difficult interpersonal situations draws upon all of these perspectives. The perspectives include: an action or behavioral component, a need for motivation to learn and perform, a motive to maintain personal security, an understanding of the cognitive processing needed to manage difficult flashpoint situations, the participation of models who can provide information about how to perform successfully, and the development of focused confidence to learn and act.

Diversity training in organizations has been criticized for not delivering on expectations to reduce prejudice and discrimination and improve organizational climate (Caudron, 1993; Flynn, 1998; Hemphill and Haines, 1997; McKee and Schor, 1999). Given these criticisms, we agree with Combs (2002), who advocates for applying multiple approaches to learning principles with a focus on self-efficacy, thus increasing the potential for the training to become relevant and valued on an everyday basis by people in organizations.

Our approach to developing the personal capacity to address diversity flashpoints relies primarily on a self-efficacy framework. Learners are encouraged to participate in the following activities:

- Review and discuss case studies (i.e., flashpoint vignettes), with the option of using role plays to enact mastery;
- View models, asking the facilitator and or participants to enact flashpoint scenarios;
- Request facilitator support for providing motivation and arousal by working with individuals at their own level while reinforcing skill development, no matter how large or small; and
- Situate the learning to enable educators to become more successful in creating a supportive and productive learning environment.

In addition, developing self-efficacy is a critical element for learning how to learn. As individuals become confident, they are more likely to continue to engage in learning despite the obstacles and challenges they may face. As individuals attempt to gain competencies in addressing diversity issues, we discover that this topic carries a strong affective component, as diversity is socially and politically charged and connected to an individual's personal identity (Combs and Luthans, 2007). As a result, enabling effective learning requires individuals to gain personal ownership of their own growth through managing their learning.

Organizational Learning

As discussed previously, learning has traditionally been examined at the level of the individual. However, a growing body of literature suggests that learning processes also apply to organizations (Argote, 1999; Argyris and Schoen, 1978; James, 2003; Schwandt and Marquardt, 2000; Senge, 1990; Yang, 2004). The idea that learning is an organizational as well as an individual phenomenon has exciting potential to leverage the talents and passion existing in any organization.

According to Schwandt and Marquardt (2000), individual learning is a necessary but insufficient condition for organizational learning. As opposed to individual learning, organizational learning is generated within the social dynamics of human interaction and individual learning. This leads to collective knowledge, understanding, and a newfound ability of the organization to adapt and change. Leveraging the social dynamic is the key to organizational learning. For example, supporting cross-departmental learning teams to address common challenges with successful practice enables individuals to develop trust and develop valued relationships across the institution in achieving broader goals.

Organizational learning depends upon a commitment by senior leaders to create an atmosphere where individuals are both motivated to learn and to share their learning with others in the pursuit of organizational goals. Traditionally, organization members have a parochial or silo view of their roles. Organizational learning requires people to shift to an enterprise-wide orientation, linking their experiences to the objectives and goals of the entire organization (Smith and Parker, 2005).

More than sponsoring training, organizational learning requires the development of structures and practices that will enable individuals, groups, and units to develop the capacity to act on the learning. Such efforts should include:

- Forming communities of practice,
- Developing dialogue skills,
- Nurturing systems that recognize the use of learning to address organizational issues,
- Aligning the organizational culture with learning and enabling people to be empowered citizens of the organization as distinct from their specialty area.

To develop a climate that supports organizational learning to address diversity flashpoints, campus leaders should consider sponsoring campus research to reveal diversity flashpoints and track changes over time as campus demographics and social climates shift (see, for example, chapter 7). Structures that support dialogue and learning communities can enhance opportunities for broader learning, especially with the inclusion of a broad representation of the campus community.

WISDOM

As we think about learning, we should heed this quote from T. S. Eliot (1963), "Where is the life we have lost in living? Where is the wisdom we have lost in knowledge? Where is the knowledge we have lost in information?" The learning we hope to achieve by addressing diversity flashpoint incidents transcends specific knowledge about the cultural characteristics of different communities, be they race, religion, nationality, ethnicity, sexual orientation, gender, class, ability, or age. This learning (see chapter 6) aims to create an orientation, or a way of thinking about approaching challenging identity difference–based situations that can lead to respectful interactions and mutual learning, including gaining specific knowledge as part of the journey. Echoing Eliot, we wish to provide a path to living a better and wiser life that is informed by knowledge.

The next chapter introduces the importance of gaining proficiency as a strong interpersonal communicator to prepare for addressing diversity flashpoint situations on the college campus.

REFERENCES

Argote, L. (1999). *Organizational learning: Creating, retaining and transferring knowledge*. New York: Springer.

Argyris, C., and Schoen, D. A. (1978). *Organizational learning: A theory of action perspective*. Reading, MA: Addison Wesley.

Babb, H. W., and Kopp, D. G. (1978). Applications of behavior modification in organizations: A review and critique. *Academy of Management Review*, 3(2), 281–92.

Baldwin, T. T. (1992). Effects of alternative modeling strategies on outcomes of interpersonal skills training. *Journal of Applied Psychology*, 77(2), 147–54.

Bandura, A. (1977). *Social learning theory*. New York: General Learning Press.

Bandura, A. (1986). *Social foundations of thoughts and action: A social cognitive theory*. Englewood Cliffs: Prentice-Hall.

Bandura, A. (1997). *Self-efficacy: The exercise of control*. New York: W. H. Freeman and Company.

Caudron, S. (1993). Training can damage diversity efforts. *Personnel Journal*, 72(4), 51–63.

Combs, G. M. (2002). Meeting the challenge of a diverse and pluralistic workforce: Implications of self-efficacy of diversity training. *Journal of Leadership Studies*, 8(4), 1–16.

Combs, G. M., and Luthans, F. (2007). Diversity training: Analysis of the impact of self-efficacy. *Human Resource Development Quarterly*, 18(1) 91–120.

Eliot, T. S. (1963). *Collected poems, 1909–1962 T.S. Eliot* (The Centenary Edition). Orlando, FL: Harcourt Brace and Company.

Flynn, G. (1998). White males see diversity's other side. *Workforce*, 78(2), 52–6.

Goldstein, A. P., and Sorcher. M. (1975). *Changing supervisor behavior*. New York: Pergamon.

Hemphill, H., and Haines, R. (1997). *Discrimination, harassment and the failure of diversity training: What to do now*. Westport: Quorum Books.

Hull, C. (1943). *Principles of behavior*. New York: Appleton-Century-Crofts.

James, C. M. (2003). Designing learning organizations. *Organizational Dynamics*. 32(1), 46–61.

Kreitner, R., and Luthans, F. (1984). A social learning approach to behavior management: Radical behaviorists "mellowing out." *Organizational Dynamics*, 13(2), 47–56.

Latham, G. P., and Sari, L. M. (1979). Application of social learning theory to training supervisors through behavior modeling. *Journal of Applied Psychology*, 64(3), 239–46.

McKee, A., and Schor, S. (1999). Confronting prejudice and stereotypes: A teaching model. *Performance Improvement Quarterly*. 12(1), 181–99.

Miller, G. (1956). The magical number seven, plus or minus two: Some limits on our capacity for processing information. *Psychological Review*, 63(2), 81–97.

Miller, G. A., Galanter, E., and Pribram, K. H. (1960). *Plans and the structure of Behavior*. New York: Holt, Rinehart & Winston.

Ormrod, J. E. (2006). *Educational psychology: Developing learners* (5th ed.). Upper Saddle River: Pearson Education.

Quoteland.com (n.d.) Retrieved March 27, 2007, from *http://quoteland.com/author.asp?AUTHORID=195*.

Rogers, C. R., and Freiberg, H. J. (1994). *Freedom to learn* (3rd ed.). Columbus: Merrill/Macmillan.

Schwandt, D. R., and Marquardt, M. J. (2000). *Organizational learning: From world-class theories to global best practices*. Boca Raton: St. Lucie Press.

Senge, P. M. (1990). The leader's new work: Building learning organizations. *Sloan Management Review*, 32(1), 7–23.

Skinner, B. F. (1950). Are theories of learning necessary? *Psychological Review*, 57(4), 193–216.

Smith, D. G., and Parker, S. (2005). Organizational learning: A tool for diversity and institutional effectiveness. In A. Kezar (Ed.), *New directions in higher education: Higher education as a learning organization,* Vol. 131. San Francisco: Jossey-Bass.

Yang, J. (2004). Qualitative knowledge capture and organizational learning: Two case studies in Taiwan hotels. *Tourism Management,* 25, 421–28.

CHAPTER 5

Communication

The unspoken dialogue between two people can never be put right by anything they say.
   Dag Hammarskjold, former United Nations Secretary-General (1990)

Interpersonal communication and its role in promoting successful outcomes on the college campus depends not only on proficiency in an academic area but also on respectful, supportive, verbal and nonverbal interaction with students. In this chapter, we review the literature of communication, culture, and intercultural communication, and extend a framework for effective interpersonal communication across difference.

COMMUNICATION: WHAT IS IT?

Imagine this scenario occurring as you stop by your departmental office to pick up mail:

As you begin looking over your mail, you notice two students waiting to speak with the receptionist. The students, first-generation Americans, are conversing animatedly in Vietnamese while they wait to be acknowledged. You overhear an administrative assistant whisper loudly to the receptionist: "I don't know why these students speak to one another in that foreign language! Don't they know they are in America and going to an American university to get educated?" The room suddenly becomes quiet. You quickly turn and notice the pained looks on the students' faces. The receptionist looks questioningly up at you.

Consider the following:

- What unspoken communication is going on here?
- How might the fundamental concern of the administrative assistant have been voiced more effectively?
- What is your role in the interpersonal communication among the students, receptionist, and administrative assistant?

The first two sections of this chapter outline the transactional and systemic functions of communication. Both are important in considering how, when, and why you might enter into such a conversation.

COMMUNICATION IS A TRANSACTION

Communication is a *transactional* process where we develop a mutually dependent relationship by exchanging symbols as we come into contact with people from cultures other than our own, such as in our neighborhoods, schools, churches, and workplaces (Cooper, Calloway-Thomas, and Simonds, 2007). Cooper and her colleagues (2007) claim that communication is symbolic, continuous, irreversible, and unrepeatable.

Communication is symbolic because we use language, both verbal and nonverbal, to create meaning. Language contains symbolic representations of shared meaning that are developed through shared interactions, some formal and some informal. For example, a professor may ask a student to contribute an opinion in a class discussion, then provide encouraging nods of the head as the student contributes his thought, raise an eyebrow as she listens, and finally give a smile when the student completes his thought. She may ask if anyone else holds a different viewpoint, or if someone would like to extend the original idea.

Communication is also continuous, connecting our past interactions with the present and the future. For example, the professor above has (or ought to have) a keen sense of who in the class is in the emerging stages of communicating their ideas, who is more practiced in volunteering contributions, and who may need guidance in listening to the contributions of others. Most college courses contain students with a range of communication ability, which must be managed by the professor so that everyone's growth is maximized.

In addition to being symbolic and continuous, communication is irreversible. Unlike the "undo" feature in a word-processing program, spoken words and their accompanying emotion are irretrievable. For example, consider the opinions expressed by public figures who speak out pejoratively about people of a particular race, ethnicity, sexual orientation, or religion (see, for example, "Hardaway apologizes," 2007).

Although these negative characterizations of others are typically followed by attempts to retract what was said (i.e., damage control), the electronic media has captured the communication of what most would consider deeply held personal prejudices (see, for example, "Summers' remarks," 2005; "Letter from President Summers," 2005).

Finally, communication is unrepeatable. That is, we cannot go back and say the same thing because communication is temporal, bounded by time. The response of a professor today has a particular effect (positive, negative, neutral) on the student who ventures a comment in her class. It evolved from a student's consideration of a particular topic, the context of which is forever changed. For example, the terms used to characterize people by skin color (e.g., colored, Black, African American) have evolved over time on the basis of changes in societal views and understandings of group affiliations.

The transactional nature of communication refers to the simultaneous, complex role-taking we engage in that goes beyond being a sender or receiver in a communicative process. That is, as one person sends a message, he or she is simultaneously receiving and interpreting messages and sending messages back. Each person in a group is doing the same, in words, voice tone, facial expressions, stance, and body language. The next part of this section describes how the perceptions of the sender and receiver in a conversation influence the outcome of a conversation.

Communication Is Based on Perceptions: Yours and Mine

Communication is continuously informed by the perceptions of the people involved. The roles perceptions play as we send and receive messages shape and often distort the nature of our intended communications.

As message initiators, we experience three types of perceptions about our communication: (1) self-perception, (2) perception of the other, and (3) perception of how the other perceives self. Imagine a communication interaction where I believe the following: I am a good conversationalist (my self-perception), you are intelligent (my perception of you), and I think you think I am a mediocre conversationalist (my perception of your perception of me).

We experience similar perceptions when we receive messages: our perception of self, our perception of the other, and our perception of how we believe the other perceives us. One could believe that: I am highly intelligent, you think I am a decent conversationalist, and I think you believe I am highly intelligent.

As expected, the closer the perceptual match between sender and receiver, the greater the likelihood communication will be effective. If our perceptions are a mismatch, as above, communication can be difficult, especially when also considering the complex elements of time, place, topic, and circumstance of the attempted communication. The next part of this section introduces these four additional structural elements that influence communication outcomes.

Additional Elements: Time, Place, Topic, and Circumstance

In addition to uneven perceptions about our communication abilities and levels of intelligence, these additional elements impact the initial communication challenge. The following scenario illustrates how the elements of time, place, topic, and circumstance complicate communication effectiveness.

> George has what he feels is an immediate need to communicate with Carrie when he sees her unexpectedly in a stairwell at the end of the day. Carrie, unbeknownst to George, is in a hurry (time), uncomfortable with a personal conversation in a stairwell (place), disturbed at being chided for how she voted on a departmental matter (topic), and/or dismayed at being accosted by an irritated (and perhaps irritating) peer on the way to a fitness class at the end of her day (circumstance).
>
> Nevertheless, Carrie pauses to listen. George, taking this as a green light for conversation, launches directly into what he wants to say, while Carrie mentally and emotionally checks out of the conversation because she is experiencing one or more of these elements. George may never recognize that the potential for clear communication is compromised by these structural challenges.

This scenario illustrates how the structural layers of time, place, topic, and circumstance can combine, causing the communication to move in a particular direction. What happens next in the stairwell conversation is guided by systemic elements of the communication process that make it a holistic process, where George and Carrie deduce meaning based on their individual patterns of verbal and nonverbal behaviors.

COMMUNICATION IS A SYSTEM

In tandem with the structural elements of communication, there are elements that are more process-oriented, making communication a dynamic system. That is, in addition to being a transaction, communication is also a *system*. It takes place within unique, interdependent systems formed when potential communicators try to interact, and it has both a *content* context (verbal, the information conveyed) and a *relationship* context (nonverbal, how the information is interpreted on the basis of the relationship between communicators).

Chen and Starosta (2005) characterize the communication system as holistic, having a social reality, and being a developmental and orderly process (2005, pp. 23–24):

- Communication is a holistic phenomenon, where people form a network of relations that give them an identity by granting them unique qualities or characteristics;
- Communication is a social reality, based on the common meanings people assign to verbal and nonverbal behaviors;
- Communication is a developmental process, where the content and social realities created by communication change and grow over time, and as such is never finished; and
- Communication is an orderly process, with human behaviors usually orderly and patterned rather than unpredictable.

We think of these components using the metaphor of dance. Given that communication is a dance, looking at how dancers become competent at their craft can shed light on how people become competent communicators. When people engage in the act of dancing, say, a tango or *pas de deux* in ballet, their partnership depends on verbal and nonverbal connections that grow over time in (hopefully) a predictable, orderly pattern. As the dance partners gain comfort with their communication system it opens the door to improving their performance on the dance floor.

The dancers' *content* context (their moves) and their *relationship* context (the way they work together as dancers) require a unique, interdependent system. They must become competent communicators to deliver a satisfying performance.

The next two sections of this chapter outline elements common to competent communication and how these relate to effective teaching and learning.

WHAT DOES IT MEAN TO BE A COMPETENT COMMUNICATOR?

Chesebro and McCroskey (2000) describe three elements of basic communication competence:

- A cognitive understanding of the communication process,
- The psychomotor capacity to produce necessary communication behaviors, and
- A positive, affective orientation toward communication.

These elements (understanding what you need to do, developing the physical capacity to do it, and wanting to do it) are the basics of communication. However, in addition to simply being understood by students, educators desire relationships with students, want to influence them, and want to be liked by them, which requires instructional and interpersonal communication competence. This realization requires us to ask what role communication has in enabling individuals to develop a relationship; simple message transmission, understanding, and feedback are necessary, but not sufficient, to achieve that broader goal. We offer the notion that real communication competence depends on an ability to build relationships, which in higher education is critical to successful learning.

As a case in point, scholars agree that communication competence across cultures depends not only on understanding the assumptions and values of our own, and others', cultural groups. Competence depends on understanding our communication style, personal style, and social style as well. In the following section we present three dimensions of individual style that generate differences in how we communicate.

WHAT DOES THIS HAVE TO DO WITH TEACHING AND LEARNING?

According to McCroskey and Richmond (1996), an educator's communication style, personal style, and social style are influenced by his or her temperament and personality. Dimensions of an individual's style such as assertiveness, responsiveness, and versatility are assumed to produce variations in communication behaviors.

- *Assertiveness* involves standing up for oneself and not letting others take advantage of you. Assertive communicators are able to initiate, maintain, or terminate conversations, according to their interpersonal goals. They talk faster and louder, use more gestures, make more eye contact, and lean into interactions.

- *Responsiveness* involves being sensitive, empathetic, and immediate when interacting with others, speaking with greater inflection, using open body gestures, and showing animated facial expressions. Responsive communicators consider others' feelings, listen to what they have to say, and recognize their needs, coming across as friendly, compassionate, warm, sincere, and thoughtful.

- *Versatility* involves being flexible, resourceful, and able to adjust, accommodate, and adapt to various situations. Versatile communicators use communication behaviors that are appropriate and effective in changing situations (e.g., adapting one's teaching behavior within one communication context such as teaching a large lecture class to another communication context such as advising students).

In addition to these temperament and personality attributes, educators need communication skills in each of these areas to be instructionally and interpersonally competent on the college campus. Most will have a dominant style ability to adjust according to the communication requirements of a situation.

According to Chesebro and McCroskey (2002), research indicates that any communication style can be successful if teachers are versatile and consistent in their interpersonal relationships with students. This requires being able to adapt to students' needs while making predictable, consistent decisions across groups of students.

For example, on the versatility dimension, we must know when to be expressive, analytical, or amiable and when not to use these strategies. On the consistency dimension, we must be predictable and consistent communicators and decision-makers so students know how to interact with us. By being versatile and consistent, our students know what to expect from us and how to communicate with us. Because college professors are professional communicators, research about how human communication functions and can be improved is central to learning and teaching.

Communicating with the purpose of developing a successful teaching/learning relationship is complex and challenging. We can learn more about effective communication if we direct our attention to other challenging communication tasks. Communicating across cultures certainly fits those criteria. More important, much is known about the topic that we can draw upon to help inform our discussion. In the next sections we discuss the nature of culture and several critical issues in communicating across culture that can enhance our understanding and practice of communication aimed at effective relationship building.

The final sections of this chapter describe the impact of culture on communication.

WHAT IS CULTURE?

While each culture has its unique characteristics, researchers tend to agree (Chen and Starosta, 2005; Cooper et al., 2007; Trenholm and Jensen, 1999) that cultural patterns share three basic components:

- *Beliefs* (ideas about the world people see as true, such as the belief of some Alaskan Eskimo families that spirits reside in the action of the northern lights);

- *Values* (things people hold dear, such as what we regard as fair or unfair, good or bad); and

- *Norms* (socially shared expectations of appropriate behavior, such as the expectation that shaking hands is a form of greeting).

These components (beliefs, values, and norms) are the filter for how we interpret verbal and nonverbal communication. We communicate on the basis of cultural patterns we have learned through communication with others in our culture.

For example, consider how we treat students in higher education when assigning a project. Do we believe they should work independently with no input from their peers or instructor? Or do we expect that the most worthwhile outcomes are usually dependent on many types of input and collaboration? Depending on what sort of academic culture we have come from, our values and norms about collaboration will vary. How we communicate these values and norms is critical when students are deciding how to respond to our instructions. Our communication of these values and norms sets the tone of the relationship between the instructor and the students and among the students. It impacts our mutual levels of trust, respect, and the commitment to work on our collective task. Culture, according to Cooper et al., (2007), affects our perceptions and how we view our world, how we communicate both in terms of verbal and nonverbal language and how that positions us in our conversations, and how we relate to others in terms of identity and kinship. We can see in Table 5.1 some examples of how culture impacts communication through the work of a number of cross-cultural scholars.

As these scholars have demonstrated through the interplay of culture on our perceptions, language, and identity, the relationship between culture and communication is clear. Culture is affected by communication, and vice versa.

WHAT IS INTERCULTURAL COMMUNICATION?

Challenges abound when people communicate across cultures. Differences in values and frames of reference create barriers to communication effectiveness. For example, differences in respect for authority or the value of power distance can lead to unnecessary deference to authority and lack of communication to individuals with higher status, or vice versa. In cultures where nurturance is valued over instrumentality, communication will tend to open with references to personal well-being and the business of work, and task accomplishment will enter into

Table 5.1
Some Impacts of Culture on Communication

Researcher/Scholars	Key Ideas
Kluckhohn, F., Strodtbeck, F. (1961)	People in all cultures face common human problems and collectively demonstrate a preferred set of solutions.
Hall, E. (1976)	Communication in different cultures varies on the importance attributed to expressing background and contextual information as part of a communication. In cultures that utilize low-context communication, the listener expects meaning to be delivered explicitly (e.g., in an engineering firm, instructions on how to operate a complex and potentially dangerous piece of machinery are explicitly described). In high-context cultures, listeners expect communication to be more subtle with social cues embedded in both the form and content of the message (e.g., In negotiations, a response of "Yes" may not mean "I agree," but may mean "I understand" and distinguishing between the two meanings involves observing multiple cues, both verbal and nonverbal).
Hofstede, G. (1997, research from 1960s and 1970s)	Work-related attitudes align with four dimensions of cultural values (individualism/collectivism, power distance, uncertainty avoidance, and masculinity/femininity). These impact communication in terms of how individuals take responsibility of ideas, are willing to be direct in communicating across hierarchies, are willing to follow rules, and focus on support versus task accomplishment.
Bond, M. (1987)	Non-Western dimensions of cultural patterns (e.g., values of thriftiness, persistence, status differences in relationships, and a sense of shame) impact communication, so issues such as saving face become integral to any communication.

conversations much later, to the frustration of people who ascribe to instrumental task accomplishment or more typically masculine values.

Principles of Mindful Intercultural Communication

Overcoming these barriers requires techniques such as active listening, conflict management and negotiation skills, feedback seeking, summarizing for accuracy, acknowledging ownership of communications, and authenticity (Gudykunst, 2003, 2005; Ting-Toomey and Oetzel,

2001). The general goal of intercultural communication is to create shared meanings where the intended message of the sender is clearly understood by the culturally different receiver.

Ting-Toomey and Chung (2005) offer eight principles to remember when seeking mindful everyday intercultural communication. We have adapted these principles to illuminate the challenges and opportunities inherent in addressing difficult interpersonal situations on campuses.

1. *People's expectations about communication vary.* This heightens the importance of exploring expectations to avoid communication blunders.

2. *Bias is normal.* Every culture has a point of view. The point of view is reflective of what people value and what issues are generally perceived to be of highest priority. Understanding how one's own point of view corresponds with the other is important if communication is going to lead to a successful relationship.

3. *Something is lost in the translation.* Being willing to look to the intent behind a communication is valuable in moving beyond words that do not have directly translatable meaning. Language carries with it legacy that is not always obvious but has significance to members of communities who are familiar with the legacy.

4. *Goals vary.* Intercultural communication involves multiple goals, depending on how the communicators define what is happening. Three types of goals are central to an intercultural encounter: (1) content goals (i.e., what do the communicators want to accomplish, and what are the potential obstacles and steps to doing so?); (2) relational goals (i.e., what are my, and the other person's, role expectations in the encounter?); and (3) identity goals (i.e., our expectations that our cultural and personal identity images will be respected in the communication interaction).

5. *Harmonizing is important.* Intercultural communication calls for understanding and accepting diverse ways of communicating (e.g., in an intercultural conflict episode, people use communication styles consistent with their values, norms, and beliefs, which must be accepted by both sender and receiver as a reasonable delivery method).

6. *People make mistakes.* Many intercultural encounters contain unintentional, well-meaning culture bumps or mistakes (e.g., avoiding or using eye contact, touch, proximity when talking), which may be misinterpreted as intentional violations of each other's cultural norms when no malicious intent existed. Acceptance of vulnerability is a key to recovering from these inevitable mistakes.

7. *Context is important.* Intercultural communication takes place in a context where patterns of thinking and behaving are interpreted by

the way physical and social settings create the mood or dynamics of the communication. Attending to and understanding the context, time, place, and setting can influence what should be said or left unsaid for another time.

8. *Change is constant.* Intercultural communication occurs in interdependent systems involving socialization, family, education, religion, politics, and the media. Culture is a dynamic web that changes and shifts as we come into contact with other individuals who are also changing and evolving. What is acceptable at one time may not be acceptable later. Being sensitive to events and the changes that follow makes a difference.

Each of these principles of intercultural communication provides a lens through which we interpret our own culture as well as interpreting unfamiliar cultural patterns. The final section of this chapter introduces a systematic approach to communicating across the myriad identity differences students bring to the college campus.

COMMUNICATING ACROSS DIVERSITY FLASHPOINTS

It is often hard to learn from people who are just like you. Too much is taken for granted. Homogeneity is fine for a bottle of milk, but in the classroom it diminishes the curiosity that ignites discovery.

Vivian Gyssin Paley (1979, p. 53)

Paley, a teacher whose career focused on guiding young learners toward appreciation of difference, makes a great point about the value of learning with and from culturally different others. Heterogeneity, in addition to its potential for igniting and sustaining discovery among people, presents communication challenges that can create defensiveness, cloud our ability to manage our communication, and lead to leaving people out of the conversation. The next chapter introduces a system for increasing communication effectiveness across difference, including the following:

- Recognize the conditions leading to a difficult interpersonal incident;
- Reflect on the critical issues and multiple perspectives surrounding the incident;
- Respond to the incident after considering various research-based response strategies; and
- Reassess the effectiveness of the action taken to address the difficult incident.

We call these "The 4 R's"—a research-based approach to mindful communication that acknowledges the transactional and systemic aspects of communication on the college campus.

REFERENCES

Chen, G. M., and Starosta, W. (2005). *Foundations of intercultural communication*. Lanham: University of Press of America.

Chesebro, J. L., and McCroskey, J. C. (2002). *Communication for teachers*. Boston: Allyn & Bacon.

Cooper, P., Calloway-Thomas, C. B., and Simonds, C. (2007). *Intercultural communication: A text with readings*. Boston: Pearson Education.

Gudykunst, W. B. (2003). *Bridging differences: Effective intergroup communication* (4th ed.). Thousand Oaks: Sage Publications.

Gudykunst, W. B. (Ed.). (2005). *Theorizing about intercultural communication*. Thousand Oaks: Sage Publications.

Hammarskjold, D. (1990). Markings: Starting with oneself, Spiritual confessions *Expository Times* Vol 101, pp. 132–134.

"Hardaway apologizes again for remarks." (2007, February 19). *The New York Times*. Retrieved April 3, 2007, from http://www.nytimes.com/aponline/sports/AP-BKN-Hardaway-Remarks.html?ei=5040&en=aa38b9).

"Letter from President Summers on women and science." (2005, January 19). *The Office of the President, Harvard University*, Retrieved April 3, 2007, from http://72.14.253.104/search?q=cache:oQvD90gMchQJ:www.president.harvard.edu/speeches/2005.

McCroskey, J. C., and Richmond, V. P. (1996). *Fundamentals of communication*. Prospect Heights: Waveland Press.

Paley, V. G. (1979). *White teacher*. Cambridge: Harvard University Press.

"Summers' remarks on women draw fire." (2005, January 17). *The Boston Globe*. Retrieved April 3, 2007, from http://www.boston.com/news/local/articles/2005/01/17/summers_remarks_on_women_draw_fire?mode=PF.

Ting-Toomey, S., and Chung, L. (2005). *Understanding intercultural communication*. Los Angeles: Roxbury Publishing.

Ting-Toomey, S., and Oetzel, J. G. (2001). *Managing intercultural conflict effectively*. Thousand Oaks: Sage Publications.

Trenholm, S., and Jensen, A. (1999). *Interpersonal communication*. Oxford: Oxford University Press.

CHAPTER 6

Understanding Diversity
Flashpoint Situations

The most important knowledge teachers need to do good work is a knowledge of how students are experiencing learning and perceiving their teacher's actions.

Steven Brookfield (2005)

*I*magine yourself entering a college auditorium for a lecture on the topic of family structures. You smile in anticipation, expecting a lecture by your sociology professor in a venue that validates your life growing up with same-sex parents. Near the end of the lecture you contribute a comment about your positive experience in a family with two mothers. Some students giggle, others laugh nervously. The professor ignores your comment and continues lecturing as if nothing has happened. Not only did your professor disregard your contribution; your peers found the mention of same-sex parents uncomfortable.

We believe that faculty development in higher education is indeed inevitable, as Saroyan and Amundsen (2004) suggest, and valuable, as Landis, Bennett, and Bennett (2004) propose. Indeed, as illustrated in the vignette, there is much to learn and understand about the inevitable challenge of intercultural communication, "the ability to communicate effectively in cross-cultural situations and to relate appropriately in a variety of cultural contexts" (p. 149).

This chapter focuses on four broad areas required to manage challenging intercultural situations: (1) the conditions that lead to diversity flashpoints, (2) the critical issues and potential effective responses to these difficult situations, (3) the array of research-based strategies that can support individuals taking action in response to flashpoint incidents, and (4) the importance of assessing the effectiveness of these actions.

To address the conditions that lead to diversity flashpoints, we have developed a system for recognizing a flashpoint, reflecting on it, responding to it, and reassessing our action. We call this the 4 R's approach to resolving difficult situations: recognize, reflect, respond, and reassess. In developing this system, we aspire to help readers form data- and research-based responses to challenging intercultural incidents.

Empirical research conducted by the authors (Garcia, Hoelscher, and Farmer, 2005) illuminates the diversity flashpoint issues (i.e., the identity-based diversity dilemma that creates a challenging interpersonal experience) and the diversity flashpoint settings (i.e., the type of behavioral situation where the incident occurred) connected with difficult interpersonal incidents on college campuses. Other sound empirical research on managing cultural conflict expands the discussion (see, for example, LeBaron, 2003; Gudykunst, 2004; and Harwood and Giles, 2005).

WHAT IS A DIVERSITY FLASHPOINT?

We define a diversity flashpoint as a potentially explosive interpersonal situation between faculty and students that arises out of identity differences. As described earlier in this book, a diversity flashpoint incident results in some or all people present recognizing a broken connection among those working together on the common task of teaching and learning. Left unaddressed, this broken connection is likely to lead to defensiveness, reduced communication, and disengagement. Addressing a diversity flashpoint incident effectively will create positive energy and lead to a more successful learning relationship.

The next section outlines our model for recognizing, reflecting on, and responding to a diversity flashpoint incident, and then reassessing the effectiveness of the action taken to address the incident.

THE 4 R'S: A MODEL FOR MANAGING DIVERSITY FLASHPOINTS

The 4 R's model creates a scaffold for tackling a diversity flashpoint incident. This is not to suggest a linear process must be followed systematically to "crack the case." Rather, it is a heuristic strategy used by effective problemsolvers who consider multiple ideas simultaneously and recursively.

Learning the model begins with reading and considering diversity flashpoint incidents written as teaching cases. The model uses diversity flashpoint incidents collected by the authors (Garcia et al., 2005) through interviews with student affairs professionals on university campuses in the United States.

The 4 R's model aims to clarify concrete steps to help faculty manage difficult interpersonal situations driven by student identity differences. In the following pages, we outline a four-step approach to addressing these challenging interpersonal situations, including recognizing what happened, reflecting on this knowledge, responding to the incident, and, finally, reassessing the actions taken.

Step 1: Recognize the Incident

Reflective practitioners begin by recognizing that there is a discrepancy between what one expects and what is actually occurring. To recognize the incident:

- Determine if it satisfies the qualities of a diversity flashpoint (i.e., difficult, potentially explosive, and identity-based);
- Identify what is happening between the people involved and describe the discrepancy between their expectations and what has occurred;
- Collect the facts without making interpretations regarding beliefs, motivation, and actions;
- Consider the case from multiple perspectives, including the people directly and indirectly involved; and
- Acknowledge you are able to see only a small part of the big picture.

For example, to recognize the diversity flashpoint incident from the sociology class described at the beginning of the chapter:

- An assertive student elects to contribute a personal example related to a sociology lecture topic; student colleagues in the group exhibit various responses including nervous laughter; the professor ignores the contribution and laughter and continues lecturing. One would expect a professor to acknowledge the contribution in some way and manage the disruptive nervous laughter in the classroom.

The next step provides strategies for reflecting on a diversity flashpoint incident when it occurs.

Step 2: Reflect on the Incident

Deliberate reflection leads to deeper understanding and can inform practice (Argyris and Schoen, 1978). One aspect of effective teaching is the ability to reflect on practice. Reflection can occur vicariously through reading and discussion of authentic teaching cases, or during an actual teaching and learning interaction. Either way, it is helpful to have a problem-solving mindset for reflection and improvement. Managing a diversity flashpoint once it has occurred requires a combination of knowledge, skill, and willingness to act. It necessitates knowing how to isolate the critical issues at the heart of the interaction, identify the range of possible responses to the situation, and predict potential consequences of each response.

Reflective practitioners frame problems on the basis of their values, experiences, and assumptions, and often invite the input of trusted colleagues. While participants may agree on the facts in a case, they may disagree on the issues involved and how to resolve them ethically and equitably. To reflect on the incident:

- Clarify what happened (i.e., what is the setting, and what are the issues involved?);
- Consider the incident from multiple perspectives;
- Explore assumptions and reasoning behind positions or viewpoints;
- Actively listen for understanding and respect multiple points of view; and
- Encourage others do the same, while owning personal feelings.

For example, to reflect on the diversity flashpoint incident in the sociology class:

- Issues involved could include the selection of an effective strategy for managing unsolicited contributions during class, understanding the responses of other students in the class, and how, when, and whether instructors should assume an ally or advocacy role in classroom settings.

The next step involves taking action when a diversity flashpoint incident occurs.

Step 3: Respond to the Incident

Responding to an incident requires considering and selecting an effective response, given your understanding of the facts. McClintock (2000) offers a taxonomy of responses to oppressive behaviors based on her work with young people in summer camps. This taxonomy represents a continuum of responses from relatively passive to more active interventions. In our view, oppressive behavior involves behavior that violates a legal or moral code and involves unfairly gaining at another's expense.

The action continuum promotes positive responses in difficult situations. It guides college teachers and students to take new perspectives on human diversity and move away from behaviors working against social justice (i.e., actively joining in the behavior or not responding when a flashpoint situation occurs). For example, educators are encouraged to model for students learning about what is behind oppressive behaviors; express their disapproval including what is oppressive about it; support others' proactive responses; and initiate proactive responses that promote understanding and valuing cultural differences in campus settings. Readers will learn how to apply a strategic decision-making model based on considering potential options, projecting potential outcomes, and choosing, using, and assessing an action strategy. That is, readers will examine: *What could I do? What should I do? What would I do? What are the multiple impacts of my strategies for action?*

Once the fact pattern of a diversity flashpoint incident is established, the search for alternative responses to the incident guides the action a person could, should, and would take. The experiences and expertise of people from different backgrounds are particularly valuable when searching for alternative plans of action after a flashpoint incident.

To search for alternatives and respond to the incident in a way consistent with the setting and issues involved:

- Generate a list of alternative responses to the flashpoint incident (i.e., if this happened to me, what could I do?);
- Examine the short- and long-term consequences of each decision for all stakeholders;
- Decide which alternatives seem most acceptable, given the needs of stakeholders (i.e., if this happened to me, what should I do?); and
- Select the most appropriate response, given this range of appropriate responses (i.e., if this happened to me what would I do?).

Table 6.1 offers examples of responses to the sociology class incident that are aimed at working toward social justice (adapted from McClintock, 2000).

The final step of the 4 R's model provides guidance on evaluating the effectiveness of actions taken to address a diversity flashpoint incident.

Step 4: Reassess the Action

Reassessing action in response to a diversity flashpoint incident requires collecting feedback from those involved in the interaction to

Table 6.1
Action Continuum for Interrupting Oppressive Behavior Regarding a Student's
Revelation in Sociology Class

Action Continuum for Interrupting Oppressive Behavior	Examples of Possible Responses to the Student's Revelation in Sociology Class
1. Educate Oneself (i.e., learn what is behind the oppressive behavior).	Learn more about family structures with same-sex parents; update lecture notes to reflect this awareness.
2. Interrupt the Behavior and Educate Those Present (i.e., express your disapproval of the behavior and explain what is oppressive about the behavior).	For example: "I notice there was laughter in the classroom in response to the comment about same-sex couples. Why did this laughter occur? Let's understand the reasons behind the laughter and its effect on our ability to understand and learn." and/or "I appreciate your contribution to the discussion on family structures. Same-sex couples have a long history of being unfairly excluded from the way families are discussed in this country. Let's not perpetuate that exclusion."
3. Support Others' Proactive Responses (i.e., recognize those who chose ally responses when the incident occurred).	For example: "Thanks to those of you who chose to respond in helpful ways to your classmate's contribution during my lecture."
4. Initiate a Proactive Response (i.e., take some kind of action that promotes understanding and valuing of cultural differences in classroom settings).	To model valuing cultural understanding an instructor might share their interest in learning: "Let's take a look at what the literature on same-sex parenting has to say about child development." Invite students to share personal stories related to growing up in families with various guardian styles (e.g., single parent, stepparents, grandparent/s, etc.).

determine the effectiveness of the management strategy or strategies used to address the incident.

This step requires re-visiting the 4 R's decision-making model and asking: What did I do, how did it affect everyone involved, what did I learn from this, and what could (would, should) I do differently next time? Readers will understand that faculty members, in addition to being content area experts, are capable of taking action in coalition with students to effect positive social change on campus. We can only improve our ability to make positive changes if we note the consequences of our actions and use this information to guide our behavior in future situations. This is the essence of learning to be more reflective, effective practitioners.

For example, to reassess a response to the diversity flashpoint incident in the sociology class:

> A faculty member must seek direct and indirect feedback from those involved in the incident. This includes the student with the same-sex parental caregivers who spoke up in class, the students who responded to his assertion, and the students who took bystander roles during the incident. Seeking direct feedback from those present would help the instructor understand how the action affected all students and how future responses could more effectively meet student needs. Seeking indirect feedback (e.g., observing whether students return to class the next day, whether they sit closer to or further from the student who spoke up in class, whether other students contribute comments in class) would help the instructor unobtrusively gauge the impact of their action.

Applying the 4 R's model on a university campus requires choosing to be an agent against systemic discrimination at both the personal and institutional levels. Prior to making the choice to identify oneself as an ally to others, university instructors must explore the effects of the privilege they hold. This includes considering a personal definition of, and motivation for, choosing to be an ally, working purposefully to understand how personal and institutional systems of oppression work, and developing skills to take responsibility for change (Kendall, 2002).

The second section of this chapter sets in motion a process for becoming skillful with using the 4 R's model for recognizing, reflecting on, and responding to a diversity flashpoint incident, and reassessing the effectiveness of the action taken to address the incident.

WORKING WITH VIGNETTES: RECOGNIZING, REFLECTING, AND RESPONDING

This section describes how to use case studies based on nationally collected diversity flashpoints to practice recognizing, reflecting, and responding to critical issues in potentially explosive interpersonal situations. The cases involve faculty members' interaction with the cultural characteristics of students (including interactions based on language and ethnicity), and feature ways to take action to address or avoid these types of situations (e.g., learning what is behind the behavior, interrupting the behavior, supporting others' proactive responses, or initiating a proactive response).

The first diversity flashpoint incident involves a faculty member overhearing a staff member's response to students speaking their native language. Read the incident and consider the steps involved in recognizing and reflecting on what happened (Step 1: Recognize). Then, consider the range of alternative responses and consider how you would respond (Step 2: Reflect, Step 3: Respond). After you've chosen a response, consider what methods you would use to clarify how your response affected each person involved (Step 4: Reassess).

Incident #1: The Xenophobic Comment

Incident: Pat Johnson, a faculty member stops by her departmental office to pick up mail. On her way into the office she notices two students waiting to talk with the receptionist. The students, first-generation Americans, are conversing animatedly in Vietnamese while they wait to be helped. Dr. Johnson hears the administrative assistant say to the receptionist: "I don't know why these students speak to each other in that foreign language! Don't they know they are in America and are going to an American university to get educated?" The room suddenly becomes quiet. Pat quickly turns and notices the pained looks on the students' faces. The receptionist looks up questioningly at Pat.

1. **Recognize:** Is this incident difficult, potentially explosive, and identity-based? Yes. Two students were conversing as they waited for assistance from departmental staff. One staff member expressed frustration to another that the students were conversing in a language other than English. The room quickly quiets; the students appear hurt. The staff person who received the comment looks to the faculty member after the incident occurs.

2. **Reflect:** What is the setting? What issues are involved? Flashpoint incident settings are the behavioral environments where the incident took place. In contrast, issues refer to the underlying point of contention that is identity-based and creates the tension in the interaction. In this incident, the setting would be 'learning management,' the management of the interactive process between and among faculty, students, and staff. The students were in the area to ask a question, to learn from staff. The issue in this incident is 'becoming an ally,' the challenge to faculty and staff to create a safe and effective learning environment for all. In this case, there is an expectation that the faculty member will step in and play a role in the situation that has developed. In reflecting on what has occurred, the faculty member should consider the assumptions and reasoning behind the positions or viewpoints of the students the administrative assistant, and the receptionist.

3. **Respond:** What alternatives for responses are realistic in this incident? Which is the most positive response? This step takes the faculty member from understanding the facts to searching for alternative responses to the incident, with a focus on selecting the most appropriate response to supporting everyone involved (Table 6.2). Consider your response given the facts presented in this incident.

4. **Reassess:** What types of direct and indirect feedback should be sought from those involved in the incident? This step seeks the opinions of the two students, the receptionist who sought faculty input, and the administrative assistant whose comment provoked the incident. Seeking direct feedback would help the faculty member understand how the action affected each person involved and how future responses could more effectively meet each of their needs. Seeking indirect feedback (e.g., observing the interaction between and among the staff members and other departmental employees, listening for whether they seek communication with the students involved, stopping in the office and listening to interactions between the staff and other students) would help the faculty member gauge the impact of their actions. In sum, this information would guide future responses to diversity flashpoint incidents.

Table 6.2 illustrates a range of potential responses to the incident you just read. As you read through the continuum, consider which responses are closest to those you thought about as you contemplated Incident #1.

Read on to try the 4 R's model on a second incident focused on a student's frustration with being expected to educate the class on issues of race.

Incident #2: A Student's Frustration with Being Asked to Educate the Class on Issues of Race

Incident: After a particularly lively discussion in a small U.S. History class, a male faculty member hears a quiet tap on his office door. He smiles as he opens the door and sees the lone African American student from the class he just taught. She enters the office and snaps, "I'm tired of how you treat me in class! You might mean well but you are making me frustrated when you keep asking me to tell the rest of the students what Black people think about things! That just sucks, if you want to know the truth!" The student looks angrily at the faculty member, then down at the carpet, fearing the worst. The faculty member's eyes widen.

Table 6.2
Action Continuum of Possible Responses to the Incident Involving a Staff Member's
Response to Students Speaking Their Native Language

Action Continuum	Possible Responses
1. Educate Oneself (i.e., learn what is behind the oppressive behavior).	Learn more about responses to assist students with varying cultural characteristics; update staff development to address these staff concerns.
2. Interrupt the Behavior and Educate Those Present (i.e., express your disapproval of the behavior and explain what is oppressive about the behavior).	For example: "I notice it was challenging to be in an area where people are speaking a language that's not familiar. When this happens it's easy to feel left out of the conversation, and also important to remember that people who speak more than one language have the right to do that." and/or "I appreciate your contribution to diversity on our campus. I also appreciate your discomfort when you hear an unfamiliar language. Both types of feelings are important to acknowledge here."
3. Support Others' Proactive Responses (i.e., recognize those who chose ally responses when the incident occurred).	For example (speaking to the receptionist): "Thanks for helping me have a chance to be part of what just happened, and to learn from it myself."
4. Initiate a Proactive Response (i.e., take some kind of action that promotes understanding and valuing of cultural differences in learning settings).	To model valuing cultural understanding an instructor might share their interest in learning a second language: "Based on what happened here I realize my efforts to learn Vietnamese would help me be a more supportive part of this campus." Invite students to share personal stories related to learning and using a second language (e.g., when and how they learned it, how they are maintaining their Vietnamese language on a campus with English as the dominant language).

1. **Recognize:** Is this incident difficult, potentially explosive, and identity-based? Yes! A student has identified a hurtful faculty behavior pattern. She has shared with the instructor her feelings of being treated as a token representative for her race. The faculty member has taken in the student's words. He considers what has happened, both in his office and in his classes to date.

2. **Reflect:** What is the setting? What issues are involved? Flashpoint incident settings are the behavioral environments where the incident took place. In contrast, issues refer to the underlying point of contention that is identity-based and creates the tension in the interaction. In this incident, the setting would be 'learning management,' the management of the interactive process between and among faculty, students, and staff. The student brought a concern to the faculty member that relates to the learning environment. The issue in this incident is 'treatment of the student as a token," treating a lone member of an underrepresented group as representative of all members of that group. The challenge to the faculty member in this incident: to hear and respond to this student's concern. In reflecting on what occurred, the faculty member should consider the assumptions and reasoning behind the positions or viewpoints of the student as a member of the class who has brought an important concern to the instructor's attention.

3. **Respond:** What alternative responses are realistic in this incident? Which is the most positive response? This step takes the faculty member from understanding the facts to searching for alternative responses to the incident, with a focus on selecting the most appropriate response to supporting everyone involved (Table 6.3). Consider your response given the facts presented in this incident.

4. **Reassess:** What types of direct and indirect feedback should be sought from those involved in the incident? This step seeks deeper understanding of the opinion of the student. Seeking direct feedback would help the faculty member further understand how the action affected the student and how he could more effectively involve her in class discussions. Seeking indirect feedback (e.g., monitoring the interaction between the student and himself as the quarter progresses, with periodic conferences along the way) would help the faculty member gauge the impact of his behavior change. In sum, this information would guide future responses to diversity flashpoint incidents.

Table 6.3 illustrates a range of potential responses to the incident you just read. As you read through the table, consider which responses are closest to those you thought about as you contemplated Incident #2.

Incident #3 involves an interaction between a graduate student and an instructor, where an unexpected comment offered by the student leads to an insensitive response from the instructor.

Table 6.3
Action Continuum of Possible Responses to a Student's Frustration with Being
Asked Repeatedly to Educate the Class on Issues of Race

Action Continuum	Possible Responses
1. Educate Oneself (i.e., learn what is behind the oppressive behavior).	Learn more about supportive ways to include all students' voices in classroom discussions and interactive activities. Seek feedback from students in minority groups in your classes to discern how they would like to make their voices heard.
2. Interrupt the Behavior and Educate Those Present (i.e., express your disapproval of the behavior and acknowledge why it is oppressive).	For example: "Thanks for helping me understand how my actions are affecting you personally." and/or "I appreciate your contributions in class and want to learn how what I can do differently to help bring out your viewpoints in class discussions without making you uncomfortable. Any ideas about how I could get better at this?"
3. Support Others' Proactive Responses (i.e., recognize those who chose ally responses when the incident occurred).	For example: "Another student in class, Ms. X, has asked me to use the phrase 'So what do you think?' to give her an opportunity to share how she feels. How does this sound to you?"
4. Initiate a Proactive Response (i.e., take some kind of action that promotes understanding and valuing of cultural differences in learning settings).	For example, "I have to say I am rather surprised by your comments. I did not intend to single you out in the way you describe. I just wanted to make sure you were included in the conversation in class. Obviously, I missed the boat on how to do this most effectively. I get a clear message on what not to do in the future. What would you like me to do instead? I want to make this work for you and the rest of the class."

Incident #3: If It Is Not from Here It Must Not Be Good

Incident: Kamala Lahiri is a student from India studying to obtain her education degree. For class, students were required to read a chapter from their textbook about effective use of technology. In class discussion the next day, Kamala raises her hand, and when the professor called on her, she said, "I feel that the information in the chapter we read last night was really dated. In fact, I noticed that this book was published three years ago, and I think some of what it says is not state-of-the-art." The professor responds, "You mean you people read books like this in your country?"

1. **Recognize:** Is this incident difficult, potentially explosive, and identity-based? Yes! A student was subjected to a degrading characterization by a professor after she expressed a critique of the course text. Both the critique and the response were exchanged in front of the rest of the class, adding to the potential harmful effect of the professor's response.

2. **Reflect:** What is the setting? What issues are involved? Flashpoint incident settings are the behavioral environments where the incident took place. In contrast, issues refer to the underlying point of contention that is identity-based and creates the tension in the interaction. In this incident, the setting would be 'learning management,' the management of the interactive process between and among faculty, students, and staff. The student approached the professor with a critique of the course text, which prompted the professor's unfair characterization of a group of people. The issue in this incident is 'using labels that marginalize,' where a person's language sets a tone that approves of disrespect for others and asserts that some people are legitimate while others are not. In this case, the faculty member's choice of words has the potential to interfere with student learning and foster an atmosphere where unearned privilege prevails. In reflecting on what has occurred, the assumptions and reasoning behind this characterization of a group of people should be examined.

3. **Respond:** What alternative responses are realistic in this incident? Which is the most positive response? This step takes the faculty member from understanding the facts to searching for alternative responses to the incident, with a focus on selecting the most appropriate response to supporting everyone involved (Table 6.4). Consider your response given the facts presented in this incident.

4. **Reassess:** What types of direct and indirect feedback should be sought from those involved in the incident? This step seeks deeper understanding of the effects of characterizing a group of people on the basis of one or more cultural characteristics. Seeking direct feedback from the student would help the faculty member further understand how the action affected her and how he could more effectively respond to her original concern: the suitability of the course text to help students meet the course objectives. Seeking indirect feedback (e.g., monitoring future interactions between the student and himself as the quarter progresses) would help the faculty member gauge the

Table 6.4
Action Continuum of Possible Responses to a Professor's Response to Student Assertiveness

Action Continuum	Possible Responses
1. Educate Oneself (i.e., learn what is behind the oppressive behavior).	Examine your biases about the behaviors, abilities, and resources available to people from parts of the world with which you are unfamiliar. Seek feedback from students in minority groups in your classes to prepare for moving from assumptions to understandings.
2. Interrupt the Behavior and Educate Those Present (i.e., express your disapproval of the behavior and explain what is oppressive about the behavior).	For example: "Yesterday in class I missed an opportunity to listen for understanding when Kamala shared her impressions of the course text."
3. Support Others' Proactive Responses (i.e., recognize those who chose ally responses when the incident occurred).	Given the facts of this case (i.e., no information about bystanders' response), no recommendation can be made.
4. Initiate a Proactive Response (i.e., take some kind of action that promotes understanding and valuing of cultural differences in learning settings).	For example: "I see I have made an assumption that is incorrect. Please share with us some of your exposure to enterprise resource planning systems from your undergraduate studies."

impact of his behavior change. As in the previous example, this information would guide future responses to diversity flashpoint incidents.

Table 6.4 illustrates a range of potential responses to the incident you just read. As you read through the table, consider which responses are closest to those you thought about as you contemplated Incident #3.

SUMMARY

This chapter introduced the 4 R's model for recognizing, reflecting on, and responding to flashpoint situations, and reassessing actions taken. We featured cases derived from our national sample of diversity flashpoint incidents.

One incident featured a student's decision to risk sharing personal information in a sociology class, resulting in a professor's decision to ignore the unexpected contribution and continue lecturing. The second incident involved a faculty member witnessing a staff person making a disparaging remark about the foreign language use of students in an office. The third incident explored a student's decision to interrupt a faculty member's unsuccessful method of encouraging classroom discussions. The fourth incident illustrated a faculty member who discounted a student's ability on the basis of her nationality. For each incident we defined and elaborated each step of the 4 R's model with emphasis on the choices a professor could consider to respond supportively on the basis of the setting and issues involved in the incident.

The next chapter introduces strategies for identifying diversity flashpoint situations on your own campus and developing realistic strategies for resolving these local incidents. Chapter 7 will illustrate an approach to: (1) collecting and categorizing local flashpoint stories, (2) creating your own case-based scenarios, and (3) critiquing potential responses to these incidents to support constructive social change on your campus.

REFERENCES

Argyris, C., and Schoen, D. (1978). *Organizational learning: A theory of action perspective*. Reading: Addison-Wesley.

Brookfield, S. (2005). Discussion as a way of teaching. San Francisco: Jossey-Bass.

Garcia, J., Hoelscher, K., and Farmer, V. (2005). Diversity flashpoints on college campuses: Understanding the topography of difficult interpersonal situations grounded in identity difference. *Innovative Higher Education*, 29(4), 275–289.

Harwood, J., and Giles, H. (Eds.). (2005). *Intergroup communication: Multiple perspectives*. New York: Peter Lang Publishing.

Kendall, F. (2002). *How to be an ally if you are a person with privilege*. Unpublished manuscript.

Landis, D., Bennett, J., and Bennett, M. (2004). *Handbook of intercultural training*. Thousand Oaks: Sage Publications, Inc.

LeBaron, M. (2003). *Bridging cultural conflicts: A new approach for a changing world*. San Francisco: Jossey-Bass.

McClintock, M. (2000). How to interrupt oppressive behavior. In M. Adams, W. J. Blumenfeld, R. Castaneda, H. W. Hackman, M. L. Peters, and X. Zuniga (Eds.), *Readings for diversity and social justice: An anthology on racism, antisemitism, sexism, heterosexism, ableism, and classism* (pp. 483–485). New York: Routledge.

Saroyan, A., and Amundsen, C. (Eds.). (2004). *Rethinking university teaching: A course design workshop and a framework for faculty development*. Sterling: Stylus.

CHAPTER

Going Local

By listening to his language of his locality the poet begins to learn his craft. It is his function to lift, by use of imagination and the language he hears, the material conditions and appearances of his environment to the sphere of the intelligence where they will have new currency.

William Carlos Williams (1883–1963) (creativequotations.com, n.d.)

This chapter provides strategies for identifying and personalizing responses to diversity flashpoint patterns on your campus. In the following pages you will learn how to:

- *Collect* local diversity flashpoint stories from your colleagues,
- *Categorize* the stories by issue and context (Garcia, Hoelscher, and Farmer, 2005),
- *Create* case-based scenarios based on these patterns, and
- *Critique* the effectiveness of these scenarios as tools for learning.

These four steps (i.e., the 4 C's) will help you contribute to healthy learning communities by generating personally and locally relevant responses to flashpoint situations.

DEVELOPING YOUR OWN STORIES TO ENGAGE EMOTIONAL AND INTELLECTUAL ATTENTION

Collecting Local Diversity Flashpoint Stories

This section provides information on how to uncover locally meaningful flashpoint situations. It discusses how interested persons can document situations involving potentially explosive interpersonal situations among faculty and students arising out of identity differences (Cushner, 2006; Flanagan, 1954; Strauss and Corbin, 1998). In the following pages you will learn about approaches to locating and listening to university personnel with whom students share their stories, as well as listening to students, particularly student leaders, about their own experience and their knowledge of other students' experiences.

Designing Your Study

There are at least three models for collecting and analyzing information about what is happening on a university or college campus: (1) top-down, (2) external evaluator, and (3) bottom-up.

(1) The top-down (or deductive) research model is a classical research method where a provost's office or faculty senate committee collects data to inform the study of a particular phenomenon, topic, or situation. In this model administrators or faculty leaders work from a general theory or question to design a study to test a hypothesis, collect and analyze the data, and create reports based on their interpretation of the data. Here, data collected is complete with few gaps in the data pattern; results are typically viewed as valid and technically correct. Often the top-down research approach is associated with a deductive approach to learning about cause effect or associative relationships.

(2) The external evaluator research model is a variant of the top-down approach and is informed by the knowledge, skills, and agendas of the person or group commissioning the study and the person directing the study. Thus, the top-down system drives the evaluator's decisions about data collection, categorization, and critique. External evaluations are viewed as a collaborative work of give and take, with data collection and interpretation directed by the external evaluator and data publication determined by the commissioning group. Typically, the external evaluator brings a standard methodology or point of view to investigate the issues informed by experiences derived at other institutions. Much like the top-down model, the external evaluator model attempts to solve problems by inferring cause-and-effect relationships from the data.

(3) The bottom-up (inductive) research model is more exploratory and open-ended, using specific observations to move toward broader generalizations and theories. Inductive studies begin with specific observations and measures, uncover patterns, formulate tentative hypotheses to explore, and result in general conclusions or theories. This method is usually informed by a person or group closely connected with the data and initiated by stakeholders interested in learning more

about something in their environment. In contrast to the top-down and external models of research, the bottom-up model is typically rather messy, where people "own" the data, work together to make sense of it, and apply the findings to their own lives. Given these characteristics, the bottom-up model is more suitable for developmental (as opposed to evaluative) activities. Rather than focusing on precision and accuracy, this model focuses on generating results that inform theory-building and action.

Our approach to learning about diversity flashpoints in higher education fits the bottom-up model. As faculty members, we examined campus life using personal interviews to reveal peoples' experience with the topic on the basis of their professional role at the university. We used the results to develop locally meaningful teaching cases and conducted faculty and staff development workshops on our campus.

Identifying Your Data Sources

We interviewed 34 student-affairs professionals on 11 college and university campuses and generated 153 stories of uncomfortable interpersonal situations involving faculty members. Our informants were university and college administrators in whom students had confided after experiencing a difficult identity-based interpersonal situation with a faculty or staff member.

We selected these university professionals because of their unique position as non-threatening support staff for students. Their non-evaluative relationship with students enables them to hear stories about student life that faculty, who have an evaluative role in the life of students, may not hear. In addition, student affairs professionals hear stories—often multiple stories—from many students; as a result, they can provide more stories per interview than can students.

In selecting your informants, consider who might be the "keepers" of the diversity flashpoint stories on your campus. How do you select these people? Like our informants, keepers typically hold a non-evaluative role on campus, have regular, deep, trusting contact with students, are good listeners and supportive probers, and can help students tell their stories honestly. Refrain from interviewing people who want to tell you stories with an agenda that discounts or distorts the student experience (e.g., people who interpret civil disagreement as a form of racism, sexism, or other oppressive behavior). Making this determination is a judgment call that draws upon your personal and professional integrity and knowledge about your campus community.

Making Your Contacts

Once you have identified a group of informants on your campus: (1) contact each person and provide a brief description of the purpose of your study, including the value to your campus of addressing difficult identity-based situations; (2) share some examples of flashpoint incidents; and (3) request an interview appointment at their convenience. We initially asked people for a half-hour of their time and were prepared to stay longer in case their story set required more time.

Our phone conversations went like this:

> Hello, this is _____ from the department of _____. Could I have a few minutes to speak with you now? (If no, ask when to call back.) I'm calling to see if I could schedule 20 minutes or so to talk with you about a special project designed to help our students. We're trying to learn about the types of difficult situations students experience when interacting with faculty and staff on campus based on students' identity differences. I'd like to talk with you because people in your position seem to hear directly from students, especially students from underrepresented groups on campus, when things aren't working out so well with faculty and staff. Before I tell you more, does this sound like something you could help us with? (If yes, continue.)
>
> The purpose of our project is to identify and address some of the "diversity flashpoint incidents" or difficult interpersonal situations that are triggered by an issue related to identity differences between students, faculty, and staff. We believe these incidents impact the learning environment of all students, and occur in the everyday lives of students, faculty, and staff.
>
> We hope that by understanding the patterns in these incidents we can better understand how diversity leads to identifiable campus challenges that can be effectively addressed by our faculty, staff, and students through focused interpersonal training and education.
>
> If you have 20 minutes or so sometime in the next few weeks, I'd love to talk with you.

Preparing for the Interview

Before the interview, become familiar with the scope of your informant's role on campus (e.g., their formal and informal roles and interactions with students, their personal interests related to identity issues, their research and conference presentation background, etc.). This will help you develop interview questions that both honor your informant's understandings of this topic and encourage them to think broadly about student stories they have heard.

Bring to the interview a commitment to listen carefully and ask clarifying questions, and a laptop or supply of paper and writing utensils. Be prepared to record the 4 W's of the incidents you hear (see Appendix III for a data-retrieval chart to help with this task):

1. Who was involved? Describe the people involved, their role relationships, and other relevant details about the identity of everyone.

2. What happened? Describe the sequence of events that characterized the difficult interpersonal situation. Remember, you are not an investigator but a co-inquirer interested in understanding (versus trying to evaluate how the situation was handled or resolved) the human experience. During the interview remind interviewees that you are seeking to understand the flashpoint incident, and not interested in passing judgment or learning about the outcome of the actions taken.

3. Where did the incident happen? Describe where it happened. Was it a public, private, or neutral place? Was it in a secure or safe environment?

4. When did the incident happen? Describe the timing or sequence of the critical events, before, during, and after the incident. What time-sensitive factors (class ending or starting, office hour drop-in time) contributed to how the incident occurred and was handled?

Conducting the Interview

Start the session by clarifying the purpose of the interview to help your informant recall the definition of a diversity flashpoint. Reiterate your purpose: you are collecting locally relevant student stories that will be rewritten as case studies for the professional development of faculty and staff. Assure your informant that, although stories may be recognizable to those involved, there will be no names or departmental affiliations attached when the case studies are created.

Listen carefully while the informant shares his/her stories, asking questions to clarify details and expand their recollection of the situation. Encourage them to share how the situation unfolded. Use active listening to verify that you are accurately noting their stories and take notes systematically to help you process the information once you start writing the cases. As the agreed-upon length of interview time nears, acknowledge this. If the stories are still flowing, offer to continue the interview if your informant has time, or to return at a later date. If the interview ends earlier than you'd expected, reassure the informant that you remain interested in learning about student stories they may recall after you leave.

At the close of the interview: (1) summarize what you have heard, making clarifications or adding additional details as needed; (2) thank your informant for helping you learn about diversity flashpoints on your campus; and (3) on the basis of their contribution, invite them to be part of a pool of people who may be called on again to contribute to future faculty development efforts in this area.

Categorizing Your Data

This section provides instructions for creating an empirically derived framework to understand the issues and contexts in which difficult interpersonal events, grounded in identity differences, occur between and among faculty and students (Garcia, Hoelscher, and Farmer, 2005). Four subsections describe how to: (1) sort the stories you have collected; (2) name the patterns in the stories; (3) identify the contexts in which groups of incidents occur; and (4) analyze the results, looking for high-frequency and high-importance results.

Sort Your Stories

Begin by transferring the stories to index cards or into an electronic database. Each story should be recorded as a data point because each card contains a unique story. Code each card by the source so you can refer back to your informant in the event you need clarification. Next, group the stories on the basis of the general issues you see emerging. For example, as you examine your cards you may notice a few stories involve challenges faculty have with accommodating students who have non-English accents. A few more might involve students who feel they had to represent their race or ethnic group in a classroom. As you encounter these stories, group them together. When a new issue emerges, start a new group. The next step of this section will help you find patterns in your diversity flashpoint stories.

Name the Patterns

Eventually, you will begin to see some patterns emerge as you accumulate your stories into groups. What primary issue is common among incidents in each group? The following issues arose in our study: accommodating student needs, treating students as tokens, student competency in the English language, comfort with difference, labels that marginalize, becoming an ally, invisibility, and intimidation.

Table 7.1
Issues and Frequency of Occurrence

Issue	Incident Count
1. Treatment of Non-Native English Speakers	(frequency) I-1.1 I-1.2 I-1.3
2. Treatment of a Lone Member of an Under-Represented Group	(frequency) I-2.1 I-2.2 I-2.3
3. Addressing the Use of Coercive Power	(frequency) I-3.1 I-3.2 I-3.3

Your study may uncover issues that are similar to or different from those in our research. Choose labels that make sense to you on the basis of the stories in each group. Eventually you will build a table similar to Table 7.1 to display your issues and the frequency of occurrence (number of stories in each group). Develop a coding system for each incident (e.g., the story about accommodating the non-English accent could be coded I-1.1, the second story I-2.2, etc.).

Once you've coded each incident by issue, the next step is to sort these same incidents by context. Step three of this section describes how to identify contexts in which your groups of incidents occurred.

Identify the Settings in Which Groups of Incidents Occur

"Settings" reflect the context in which significant human interaction occurs in the psychosocial environment of higher education. In our study, we identified the following settings: expectations for learning, curriculum and content, learning management, and assessment.

Your study may find settings that are similar to or different from those in our research. Again, choose labels that make sense to you on the basis of the stories in each group. Eventually you will build a table similar to Table 7.2 to display your settings and the frequency of occurrence (number of stories in each group). Develop a coding system for each incident (e.g., the first story about accommodating the non-English accent happened in the learning management setting and could be coded S-1.1, the second story S-2.1, etc.).

Table 7.2
Issues and Settings and Frequency of Occurrence

	Setting			
Issue	S-1	S-2	S-3	S-4
I-1	Freq (I-1.2, S-1.1)	(I-1.1, S-1.2)		
I-2	(I-2.1, S-2.1)	(I-2.2, S-2.2)		
I-3				
I-4				

The next step of this section lays out some ideas for analyzing the data patterns, looking for incidents of high frequency and importance.

Analyze Your Results

In our interviews we identified 153 separate diversity flashpoint incidents. Our research team independently reviewed each incident and sorted them into categories, reserving a holdout sample to assess the completeness of the sample of interviews. We then compared the results of our respective sorting and developed two types of categories: (1) categories describing the nature of the primary issue inherent in each incident, and (2) categories describing the setting in which the incident occurred. This resulted in a matrix with eight categories of issues and four categories of incident settings (see Table 1.1 in Chapter 1), similar to your version of Tables 7.1 and 7.2.

To test the completeness of our sampling technique, we then independently reviewed a holdout sample (10 percent of the total sample) to see if any new issues or settings emerged. This review did not reveal any new categories, so we were able to include these incidents in the original sample and confidently close the data-collection portion of this project.

If we had discovered stories from the holdout sample that did not fit any of our existing categories, we would then need to go out and collect more stories to assure we had a complete picture of the phenomenon.

Your data analysis will result in understandings directly relevant to your campus. Once you identify these understandings, you will be ready to develop case-based scenarios for local professional development. We suggest that you examine your data to identify patterns where issues and or settings are associated with a large number of incidents. These occurrences signify important areas of concern regarding local challenges in diversity climate. In addition, some incidents may be reported infrequently but have the potential for harm; these should also be noted, as should any incident that is of material significance, even if it is a relatively rare event.

Next you will learn how to examine your stories and develop some of them as teaching cases.

CREATING CASE-BASED SCENARIOS

This section describes how to develop short, case-based scenarios for recognizing and responding to the facts from locally collected diversity flashpoint incidents. This requires examining your local data set and considering which types of incidents are most compelling to feature in professional development opportunities on your campus.

Selecting Stories for Scenarios

Choosing stories to feature requires identifying relevant themes or issues related to the current climate on your campus. One way to do this is to consider which types of issues are most prevalent in your data. Another is to consider which incidents hold the greatest potential for harm.

Consider, also, which incidents hold potential as interesting, instructive cases that will engage the 4 R's model outlined in the previous chapter. When you use the cases you will be guiding colleagues to recognize what happened in the incident, reflect on this knowledge, respond to the incident, and, eventually, reassess the actions taken.

Writing Your Own Case-Based Scenarios

Writing case scenarios (see Appendix H) requires changing the names and settings in the original story and broadening the context of the story to protect the people involved while retaining the issue and context of the situation. The scenario should be clear, concise, interesting, and believable while maintaining the original conflict situation (Cushner, 2006).

Our approach to preparing case scenarios starts with identifying the theme or issue we want to focus on and developing a simple paragraph to describe the setting (where did it happen), the actors (who was involved), and what happened. Then we develop a short set of questions to help readers do four things:

- Identify the critical issue or problem that occurred,
- Consider the issue or problem from multiple points of view,

- Forecast potential appropriate responses to the issue or problem, and
- Speculate about possible consequences of each response for everyone involved (Ginsberg and Wlodkowski, 2002).

In sum, these are the steps of our 4 R's model. To work toward these goals, first state the facts of the case in a brief synopsis. Then develop a simple set of questions to guide participants to identify the critical issues and discuss how the issues relate to their own experience. Next, create a few probing questions to help participants identify their personal responses to the case (e.g., potential assumptions of people involved in the incident, possible motives for people's behavior, pros and cons of people's responses). Examples of these types of questions are available in the cases in Appendix H.

As you create scenarios, remember that a primary goal is to help people explore assumptions behind being an ally for others, with an emphasis on social justice and learning for all. This requires defining the term, understanding the difference between being supportive and being an ally, being clear about one's motive for becoming an ally to a particular person or cause, exploring the expectations and boundaries related to being an ally, and understanding the varying roles that people with privilege can play (Kendall, 2003).

The next section describes how to critique the effectiveness of your teaching cases and improve their use as professional development tools.

CRITIQUING THE EFFECTIVENESS OF YOUR SCENARIOS

This section provides information on evaluating the effectiveness of your written scenarios to address local diversity flashpoint situations. For example, is the situation depicted in the scenario "too hot to handle?" Does it surface the issues? Is it believable? Is it likely to stimulate constructive discussion of the issues? In other words, the purpose of the case scenario is to stimulate thoughtful, reflective discussion around using the 4 R's model with "legs" both in the lived community of the people it happened to and the people considering it. We offer the following considerations in evaluating scenarios. Does the scenario create the appropriate amount of discomfort? Is it believable? Is it locally relevant? How does the scenario fare in a test run?

Becoming Comfortable with Discomfort

The scenario must be credible, containing affective elements that are engaging to consider but do not threaten or immobilize people as "too hot to handle." In essence, the case must push people to the edge of their discomfort while also being within their safety zones (i.e., zone of proximal development) as faculty members and staff. We want to have cases that lead to these outcomes.

Creating a Circle of Critical Friends

Your locally developed cases, once drafted, should be piloted among a representative sample of the target community (critical friends). This group should be encouraged to provide critical feedback about the case that helps you determine that the case is realistic (i.e., reasonable, highly-charged). For example, if the case is judged as ho-hum or boring, you would discard it.

Developing Local Validity

The attributes of your campus community must be considered when developing stories to develop into cases for local use. To the extent that your campus is distinctive, the selection and development of scenarios for use need to conform to the sensibilities of the community. Consider the people working on your campus (e.g., the custodians, the campus security officers, the provost, the compensation analysts, food service providers, faculty, printing and publication services, coaches, residence life advisors). Imagine how these campus employees might respond to the same scenario. On some campuses, the response might be very uniform. On others, their occupational status might impact the degree to which a scenario is relevant to them. Your mission, should you choose to accept it, will be to determine if your scenarios are suitable for the entire campus community or not. If not, then you will need to match scenarios to your different audiences.

REFERENCES

Creativequotations.com (n.d.), Retrieved September 26, 2007, from http://creativequotations.com/one/522.htm.

Cushner, K. (2006). *Human diversity in action: Developing multicultural competencies for the classroom.* Boston: McGraw-Hill.

Flanagan, J. C. (1954). The critical incident technique. *Psychological Bulletin,* 51, 327–358.

Garcia, J., Hoelscher, K., and Farmer, V. (2005). Diversity flashpoints on college campuses: Understanding the topography of difficult interpersonal situations grounded in identity difference. *Innovative Higher Education,* 29(4), 275–289.

Ginsberg, M., and Wlodkowski, R. (2002). *Creating highly motivating classrooms for all students: A schoolwide approach to powerful teaching with diverse learners*. San Francisco: Jossey-Bass.

Kendall, F. E. (2003, May). *Pre-work to becoming an ally to people of color if you are a person with white privilege*. Paper presented at the annual meeting of the National Conference on Race and Ethnicity in Higher Education (NCORE), San Francisco.

Strauss, A., and Corbin, J. (1998). *Basics of qualitative research: Techniques and procedures for developing grounded theory* (2nd ed.). Thousand Oaks: Sage Publications.

CHAPTER

Anticipating Future Challenges

There is nothing more difficult to take in hand, more perilous to conduct or more uncertain in its success than to take the lead in the introduction of a new order of things.

Niccolo Machiavelli (1469–1527) (Bergin, 1947)

WE MAKE THE ROAD BY WALKING

This book originated from a commitment to inspire compassionate communication across the identity differences of university students, staff, and faculty. Our interviews with student services colleagues across the United States surfaced a disparity between interest and action: although faculty and staff report interest in supporting students' identity differences, many struggle to translate this interest into action.

Like the authors, most faculty and staff received little training aimed at competently supporting the cultural attributes of students before accepting university positions. For those students with a constellation of cultural characteristics similar to our own, we are somewhat adept at noticing what is happening in a particular situation, considering how to address unexpected situations, and acting in a reasonably helpful way. In situations involving students whose characteristics vary moderately or dramatically from our own, we tend to be less prepared to recognize what's going on and therefore less likely to respond supportively. Though we may be interested, we often lack the knowledge, skills, and attitudes necessary to take positive action on behalf of the people entrusted to us on our campuses: our students.

We developed this book to bridge the gap between interest and action. It meets a distinct need defined by the American Council on

Education (ACE) at its 2006 annual conference, where access to, and success within, higher education was a national imperative: "What are we doing as leaders of our community to ensure both access to our institutions *and success within them* [italics added]? What can we learn from one another?" (ACE, 2006).

On the one hand, colleges and universities are documenting steady gains in recruiting underrepresented populations onto their campuses (Milem, Chang, and Antonio, 2005). On the other hand, access to college depends on human capacity building to ensure the opportunity for all students' college success (ACE, 2006). In our opinion, a critical aspect of capacity building involves diversity flashpoint training for university staff, faculty, and administrators.

This chapter builds a case for diversity flashpoint training in three sections:

- A summary of the origins and development of the diversity flashpoint framework leading to developing locally authentic flashpoints,
- A call to become a builder in your organization, and
- A roadmap for taking diversity flashpoint competencies back to work.

The metaphor of a roadmap is purposeful, given the tendency for this work to offer unexpected obstacles and challenges along the way: unfamiliar terrain, constant construction, detours, disappearing lane lines, falling rocks, mudslides, and other debris, to name a few. However, we believe the value of successfully navigating personal identity incidents pays dividends that temper the challenges of relationship-building across identity differences.

The first section of this chapter summarizes the origins and development of the diversity flashpoint framework.

DIVERSITY FLASHPOINT FRAMEWORK: ORIGINS AND DEVELOPMENT

Understanding Diversity Flashpoint Situations

Our research began at home on the campus of Western Washington University, and it led us to examine difficult interpersonal situations related to identity difference on eleven other U.S. campuses. We characterized these flashpoint incidents by behavioral setting and issue, noting two types of patterns: (1) the conditions under which the predominance of incidents occurred; and (2) the representation of particularly damaging interactions that occurred—those from which it is less likely students are able to recover and remain in school (Garcia, Hoelscher, and Farmer, 2005).

On the basis of these patterns of occurrence, we selected representative flashpoint incidents and developed case-study vignettes to bring to life the lived experiences, influenced by identity difference, of university students. We piloted the case studies with colleagues at professional conferences across the United States and at faculty and staff development sessions on the Western Washington University campus. From these pilot sessions, we evolved a framework for understanding diversity flashpoint situations (i.e., the 4 R's system), providing informed, inclusive steps that professionals can use to:

- Recognize what is happening in a particular situation,
- Reflect on possible ways to address the incident,
- Respond in an informed, supportive way, and
- reassess the outcomes of the intervention.

As outlined in Chapter 7, applying this system to locally collected student stories requires collecting and categorizing the stories from your campus, creating your own case-based scenarios, and critiquing their effectiveness on your campus.

Developing Locally Meaningful Cases

Because campus climates and student identity differences vary widely, we encourage readers to apply this framework locally by uncovering meaningful flashpoint situations from their campuses. Our system for collecting and developing stories to engage emotional and intellectual attention includes four types of strategies:

- Collect local diversity flashpoint stories from your colleagues (i.e., design your study, identify your data sources, make your contacts, prepare for your interview, conduct the interview);
- Categorize the stories by issue and context (i.e., sort your stories, name the patterns, identify the settings in which groups of incidents occur, and analyze your results);
- Create case-based scenarios based on these patterns (i.e., select stories for scenarios, write your own case-based vignettes, see Appendix H for a set of sample vignettes); and
- Critique the effectiveness of these vignettes as tools for learning (i.e., become comfortable with discomfort; create a circle of critical friends; develop local validity).

Gaining access to campus stories and working with them to improve the climate for students on your campus takes time, energy, and conviction. It requires becoming so comfortable with your conviction that you are will-ing to try, fail, and revel in small victories on your college or university campus. Recognizing and responding to diversity flashpoint incidents requires leaders who focus and follow through in the spirit of Antoine de Saint-Exupery, who believed, "you give birth to that on which you fix your mind" (as cited in Porras, Emery, and Thompson 2007, p. 105).

The next section offers advice for campus administrators, staff, and faculty committed to the personal growth necessary to lead diversity efforts on their campuses.

BECOMING A BUILDER IN YOUR ORGANIZATION

What makes eternally successful and extraordinary organizations endure? According to Porras, Emery, and Thompson (2007), these organizations are led by builders:

> People whose beginnings may be inauspicious but who eventually become defined by their creativity ... who feel compelled to create something new or better that will endure throughout their lifetime and flourish well beyond ... who see themselves simply as people trying to make a difference doing something that they believe deserves to be done with or without them, and they recruit the team—build the organization—needed to get it done. Great organizations can be a dividend of this process, but enduring institutions seem to be more of an outcome of the Builder's mindset than a goal in and of itself. (p. 5)

Your organization is likely to employ others like you who are creative and committed to doing what needs to be done to build relationships between and among people who are different. This is the key: finding your own will to create change and then finding others with the same dream. In this section we discuss how new competencies create oppor-tunities and challenges in one's professional career that are addressed, in part, by opening yourself to growth.

Knowing Yourself: An Awareness Model

In Chapter 5 we describe the transactional (i.e., roles and percep-tions) and systemic (i.e., the context and content) characteristics of communicating with others. We present an example of a chance encounter in a stairwell between two faculty members, one of whom (George) asserted his need to be heard while failing to understand cer-tain constraints faced by his female colleague (Carrie). As George attempted to draw Carrie into a discussion, he had no clue that she was fuming, not only at being cornered in a public place and engaged

Figure 8.1
Personal Awareness Model

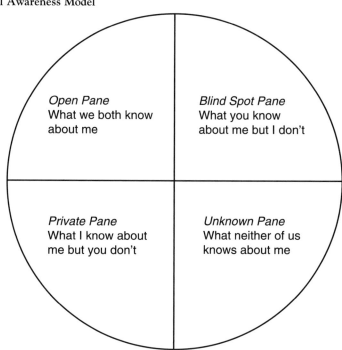

Open Pane
What we both know
about me

Blind Spot Pane
What you know
about me but I don't

Private Pane
What I know about
me but you don't

Unknown Pane
What neither of us
knows about me

Source: Adapted from Raines & Ewing (2006).

in discussion about a controversial issue, but also because she was in a hurry to get to an appointment. In this case, George was blind to his unreasonable expectations during this chance encounter. His blind spot kept him from interacting effectively with Carrie.

The model in Figure 8.1 (Personal Awareness Model) for enriching personal perspectives presents a framework for analyzing the interaction between two people, George and Carrie. The model can also help examine interactions between and among university administrators, staff, and students. It is an adaptation by Raines and Ewing (2006) of the Johari Window model for showing personal awareness (Luft and Ingham, 1955). A four-paned window divides personal awareness into four different types, each in a separate quadrant:

- The *open* pane (top left) symbolizes easily observed aspects of your personality known to yourself and others (e.g., physical features, dress, voice, vocabulary);
- The *private* pane (lower left) represent personality aspects you know about yourself and conceal from others (e.g., your aunt is in jail for

forgery, you speak fluent Japanese but you keep this hidden because you anticipate your colleagues' bias against Japanese-Americans);

- The *blind spot* pane represents things others know about your personality, but about which you are unaware (e.g., George doesn't know that his colleagues fear conversations with him because his method of approach ignores their reality; he doesn't know that he holds gender biases and that his supervisors are discussing ways to guide him toward addressing these biases as a teacher and colleague);

- The *unknown* pane shows what neither you nor others know about you (i.e., aspects of your personality yet to be discovered and used, such as a talent for mediating disputes between angry constituents, or for developing a believable storyline for a best-selling novel).

The Personal Awareness Model depicts known and unknown dimensions of ourselves. It is crucial that we become aware of what we and others both know about ourselves, and of our blind spots (what others see but we don't), areas that are unknown to ourselves and others, and what we know but others do not (Raines and Ewing, 2006).

Point of View and Perspective

As a campus leader, clarifying your personal perspective or point of view can lead to creating useful connections with others. In fact, a diversity flashpoint mentor assumes the responsibility of expanding the "open" pane for others on campus. This involves, among other things, being able to see situations from points of view well beyond the first person. The next part of this section outlines three points of view: first person (seeing an interaction from our own viewpoint), second person (seeing it from the other's point of view), and third person (seeing it from an observer's viewpoint).

First-Person Perspective

The Personal Awareness Model starts with a strong first-person perspective (seeing what you see, hearing what you hear, feeling what you feel, and knowing what you know). To strengthen this perspective, it is important to honor your own feelings and perspectives as fully as you do others, understanding your biases, no matter how illogical or politically incorrect they seem. Paradoxically, when you are fully aware of your own experience you can find your way back to being objective enough to connect with others who are different from you.

For example, as a campus leader you may notice your positive bias toward people who share your political beliefs and also find it intriguing (maybe even informing) to listen to podcasts featuring viewpoints of "the other side." Or you may own your biases about a particular topic or event publicly in administrative meetings while encouraging others to do the same. When campus leaders model such openness colleagues have the opportunity to do the same.

This is one of the first steps in working with difficult interpersonal situations: recognizing what's happening. It requires collecting the facts, considering as many potential explanations as possible for what has occurred, and acknowledging you are able to see only a small part of the bigger picture.

Second-Person Perspective

This is the point where you can see a situation through others' eyes by taking on the other person's personal history, beliefs, and values. You strengthen this perspective with keen observation skills that notice the other person's posture, gestures, and voice, in the same way a method actor connects with her character. It is useful when you aim to understand someone more fully and deepen rapport.

For example, as a leader you can move beyond merely inviting people to share their viewpoints; you can help develop linkages between your own and your colleagues' personal stories and the stories of students at your institution.

This correlates with the second step in addressing a flashpoint incident: reflecting on what each person brings to a situation, considering multiple perspectives, and exploring assumptions and reasoning behind peoples' positions or viewpoints. This is active listening at its best—listening for understanding and respecting multiple points of view, and encouraging others do the same while owning their personal feelings.

Third-Person Perspective

This perspective involves seeing a situation from a distance as an observer and letting go of the emotional intensity involved, especially when a situation seems stuck or irreconcilable. It is most useful when emotions run high, and gives people a chance to gather their thoughts and insights in a rational way to balance opposing feelings. Leaders use this perspective to help identify their part in a difficult situation (i.e., to seek alternative explanations and identify new options).

For example, because you are a campus leader you routinely search for alternatives to situations and respond in a way consistent with the settings and issues involved. This correlates with the third step in addressing a flashpoint incident: responding, which requires considering and selecting an effective response given your understanding of the facts.

The action continuum presented in Chapter 6 promotes positive responses in difficult situations, where campus leaders take new perspectives on human diversity and move away from behaviors that work against social justice. Here you have an opportunity to model for your colleagues how to learn about what is behind oppressive behaviors; how to express your disapproval, including what is oppressive about it; how to support others' proactive responses; and how to initiate proactive responses that promote understanding and valuing cultural differences. In Chapter 6, we describe how to apply a strategic decision-making model based on considering potential options; projecting potential outcomes; and choosing, using, and assessing an action strategy.

Once the fact pattern of a diversity flashpoint incident is established, the search for alternative responses to the incident guides the action a person could, should, and would take. The experiences and expertise of people from different backgrounds are particularly valuable when searching for alternative plans of action after a flashpoint incident. This process follows the classic problem-solving model that many of us use every day:

- Generate a list of alternative responses to the flashpoint incident (i.e., If this happened to me, what could I do?);
- Examine the short- and long-term consequences of each decision for all stakeholders;
- Decide which alternatives seem most acceptable, given the needs of stakeholders (i.e., If this happened to me, what should I do?);
- Select the most appropriate response, given this range of appropriate responses (i.e., If this happened to me what would I do?).

Taken together, these three perspectives (first person, second person, and third person) form the basis for considering your own role in a particular situation, what others bring to the situation, and what the situation looks like to an outside observer.

In addition to knowing themselves, three types of personal attributes can aid diversity flashpoint mentors in their journey toward encouraging their university colleagues to publicly support student identity differences. They are meaning, thought style, and action style.

Three Essential Elements for Lasting Success

Organizational researchers (Porras, Emery, and Thompson, 2007) have found three essential elements that come into alignment in the lives and work of builders: meaning, thought style, and action style. Figure 8.2

Figure 8.2
Aligning Your Thought and Action to Pursue What Matters

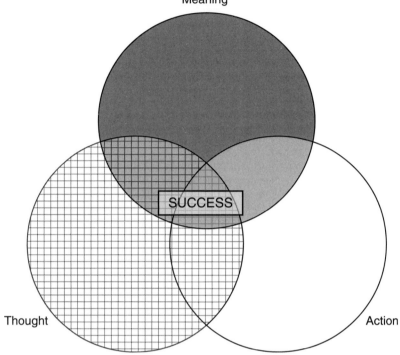

(Aligning Your Thought and Action to Pursue What Matters Most) illustrates the interrelationship among these essential personal attributes for lasting success: meaning, thought style, and action style.

- Meaning: What you do must matter deeply to you, be something you are willing to recruit other people to do, and that you will do despite criticism.

- Thought style: Builders have a highly developed sense of accountability, audacity, and responsible optimism. They have talent and perhaps a highly developed intellect, but they also need a style of thinking that supports special accomplishments.

- Action style: Enduringly successful people turn meaning and thought into action without needing conditions to be perfect. It's about the pleasure of the work, not the perfect picture.

According to Porras, Emery, and Thompson (2007), builders manage their thoughts efficiently and then "take relentless action in pursuit of what matters to them" (p. 27). They believe the great opportunity in life and work is to make that target in the center as big as possible by bringing all three circles together and increasing the degree of overlap.

To move toward greater meaning in your life on the basis of alignment of your thoughts and actions, you must become keenly aware of what matters in your life. From there, building your thoughts and actions can support your definition of meaning. Builders do well with ambiguity, though human nature craves certainty, detailed plans, and strong odds of success.

Meaning First, Method Second

Belief that we have to do something comes first; knowing how to do it comes later. When John F. Kennedy was building support for a lunar launch, he and scientists of the time had only partial knowledge of how to get there and back. What they were able to do was capture the imagination and passion of the country to "swallow public failures, learn from them, improve, and eventually prevail through thousands of tiny steps" (Porras, Emery, and Thompson, 2007, p. 175).

Responsible Chutzpah

Rather than pursuing a college degree, Michael Dell had the bold vision to sell computer equipment out of his bathtub at the University of Texas, Austin. In addition to being comfortable with ambiguity and having the passion to pursue a dream, Dell possessed "chutzpah," the nerve and audacious accountability that he could do what he set out to do, despite the opinions of others. His company succeeds today by setting clear, measurable goals driven by the needs of their consumer base.

In the next part of this section, we present strategies for knowing others and connecting across differences.

Knowing Others

National Public Radio's award-winning talk-show host Terry Gross is widely known as a masterful communicator across difference, able to bridge the gap between listeners and the very diverse people she interviews. She does this by connecting her guests' personal lives and their work, and she broadcasts the stories she uncovers in an unhurried, conversational style characterized by attitudes and skills developed over a long career. Her success derives from four foundational starting points: meticulous background research to understand the lives of her guests; a genuine acceptance of different beliefs, values, and lifestyles; a clear focus on the other person; and mindful listening skills (Raines and Ewing, 2006). Terry Gross's ability to connect so effectively with others stems from her attitude that it's not about her, it's about her guests.

Gross's skills must be transposed to the college campus by department chairs, college deans, provosts, and presidents. It's not about us; it's about our students and other stakeholders, including students' families, university alumni and other community supporters, and all university employees. However, our students represent the next generation of thinkers and citizens to whom we are most responsible. Although it is true that without our students we would have no jobs, it is also true that without students we would be robbed of the intellectual vitality that is integral to education. Appreciating our students leads us toward intercultural communication that is genuine and mindful in its focus on others. As leaders and mentors, a focus on the centrality of students to our academic mission is critical.

One Size Does Not Fit All: Getting Beyond the Golden Rule

Another aspect of knowing others involves recognizing that one size does not fit all. That is, treating someone the way we would like to be treated might work when the other's cultural characteristics are aligned with ours, but is likely to cause a disconnect when the other person is different. Assuming everyone sees the world in the same way is at the heart of diversity flashpoint situations. Recognizing this, and working actively to understand and surface different ways of thriving in the world, is critical. Businesses do this routinely by creating marketing plans to appeal to consumers. Educational institutions must do the same by tuning into the value systems of students and families.

The Titanium Rule

Raines and Ewing (2006) refer to the Titanium Rule: people connect via similarities, and connecting with people from whom we differ requires identifying and increasing our similarities. They observe that we cannot change things like our birthplace, skin color, or our ethnicity, but we can find ways we are similar and be observant of peoples' posture, gestures, eye contact, voice tone, language patterns, expectations, and beliefs. Matching even one of these characteristics helps shift our behaviors toward empathy, awareness, and understanding, and "finding ways, based on knowing what we know about another person, to make stronger connections by adapting, experimenting, and changing the way we do things" (p. 34).

The following portion of this section presents five core principles that university leaders can use to promote operating effectively across difference (Raines and Ewing, 2006): find a bridge, be curious, expect the best, recognize individual cultures, and expect nothing in return.

Each principle is translated toward becoming a diversity flashpoints mentor by suggesting ways to adapt your own style to enter the worlds of colleagues.

Connecting across Difference: Five Core Principles

1. There's Always a Bridge

We can always find common ground with others, no matter how different we are. Richard and Michele Streckel (n.d.) demonstrate this with their Milestones Project, a nonprofit foundation bringing them into contact with children, parents, and grandparents of all colors and belief systems around the world. Their photographic work "Celebrating Childhood around the World" aims to reduce hatred by focusing on similarities among children of various cultures at milestones in their lives (http://milestonesproject.com/index.php/big_picture).

Find the Bridge.   Locating commonality in the face of difference requires peering deeply into the heart and mind of the other. Some people liken this to looking through a window versus looking into a mirror. Finding what you agree upon, especially with a person with whom you previously decided you have nothing in common, can be stimulating and rewarding. Guiding university students, faculty, and staff toward areas of agreement requires visible and credible leadership in publicly modeling the value of finding common ground, in terms of making offers to communicate and being persistent about potential for bridge building.

Offers.   It starts with putting forward a piece of information about you: making a bid or an offer to communicate with another person. We may do this casually in elevators, while waiting in long lines, or while sitting in the bleachers at university sports events, and we can usually depend on our offer being accepted. You might make an offer that reveals something about yourself: "How about this wind? It reminds me of how miserable it was riding the bench with my high school soccer team." The soccer dad sitting next to you might build on the offer with an empathetic response, "I know what you mean. I still have splinters from my days on the bench during high school football." Or, he could block your offer and change the subject: "Did you see the Lehrer News Hour last night?"

Persistence.   In addition to being facile with making bids or offers to discover commonality, strong connectors stay constructive and focused on the outcome rather than judging or feeling self righteous. If you believe there is always a bridge, you can cross cultural divides—even with a smile.

2. Curiosity Is Key

Curiosity about others opens an emotional and intellectual door that, once open, leaves less room for judgment or self-righteousness. Rather, curious minds look for the bridges, the connections to others, and the opportunities to grow and change on the basis of new information.

Build Curiosity. An inquisitive nature leads people to seek information, read up on unfamiliar topics, and look for alternative opinions, all activities that lead to relationship building. This is one of the keys to navigating flashpoint situations—being willing to enter into and create bonds with others. Curious people take advantage of unexpected situations by paying attention to what is happening because each interaction is a unique chance to learn from others.

Neurologists believe curiosity increases connections inside the brain (Taflinger, n.d., as cited in Raines and Ewing, 2006). "Investigating the unusual creates new neurological pathways. The more pathways, the more possible responses to stimuli; the more possible responses, the greater likelihood of a proper response to another novel situation. Curiosity strengthens these learned responses" (p. 56).

Connecting with people whose cultural characteristics vary from ours gives us chances to practice open-mindedness and flexibility, and to learn from everyone and everything we encounter.

3. What You Assume Is What You Get

Effective communicators approach every person and situation, no matter how different, expecting the best. They seek out people who differ and presuppose that everyone has valuable contributions to make.

Assume the Best. A wise person once made an astute observation: whether you believe you can or you believe you cannot, either way you are right. As theorists point out, there is a strong relationship between goals and performance (Locke, Latham, and Erez, 1998). Our expectations shape our behavior, which makes it reasonable to focus our assumptions on the outcomes we desire. The self-fulfilling prophesy is very real. For example, if we assume we will lose a golf match, we are more likely to lose; if we assume we will win, the odds of winning increase. If we assume we have the skills to model a proactive response to an emerging flash-point situation, we are likely to feel more confident in doing so. Positive intent can mitigate the indecisiveness we feel when we decide to inter-rupt a conversation we anticipate will be hurtful to one or more parties present. When we change our focus from worrying about failing to identi-fying what we can do to help personal learning take place, we strengthen our resolve to take a small step. Small steps lead to small gains; small gains, compounded, can change the world.

4. Each Individual Is a Culture

We are all different, each with a unique set of cultural attributes. Through knowing two cultures well, and being a great and responsive listener, Hector Orci, founder of La Agencia de Oro & Asociados, developed a career connecting the Latino consumer with products and ideas. When interviewed by Terry Gross, Orci attributed his success to the guidance of one of his mother's sayings: "Cada cabeza es un mundo [every head is a world]."

Acknowledge Individual Cultures. Knowing people as individuals (versus categorizing people by their constellation of cultural attributes) takes time, commitment, and a belief in the value of difference. If you routinely treat people with dignity no matter how different they are from you, and treat every interaction as a chance to learn and grow, your potential to model this for students and other learning colleagues will soar. Indeed, there is much to appreciate about difference.

5. No Strings Attached

Great people don't necessarily expect reciprocity. That is, Terry Gross does not necessarily expect great listening or accolades from her interviewees. Richard and Michele Streckel are kind and generous to the people they meet but are not devastated when treated differently. Rather than taking it personally, they take notice, assume there's a rea-son, try to learn what caused the reaction, and become even more curi-ous, which leads to more success in the future.

Ignore the Strings. Diversity flashpoint mentors connect compas-sionately with people different than they are and should not expect to be sought out themselves. This focuses your actions solely on the fact that acting compassionately is a gift in itself.

Taken together, these principles promote a core set of beliefs, expectations, and assumptions for connecting across difference.

Modeling these five principles with faculty, staff, students, and members of the public one encounters is important to promoting responsible management of diversity flashpoint situations.

The final section of this chapter describes the challenges one might encounter in moving along the path of promoting diversity flashpoint competencies. In particular, we will point out the inevitable challenges one will receive from others who do not recognize the impact of these flashpoints on the learning climate. We will extend our discussion to strategies for building personal and professional support around this work.

TAKING IT BACK TO WORK: BUILDING YOUR CAPACITY FOR DIVERSITY FLASHPOINTS LEADERSHIP

In the introduction to this chapter, we used the phrase "make the road by walking" to characterize the process of deliberate study and action over time (Ambrosio, 2003). University professionals can begin the journey toward recognizing, reflecting on, and responding to diversity flashpoints in myriad ways. We are likely to view as cumbersome and uncomfortable the process of getting involved, being an ally, speaking up, or taking a stand when we witness (or initiate) a diversity flashpoint incident. But small steps can lead to big gains, for our students and ourselves.

In this final section we describe how engaging in this approach to addressing diversity flashpoints will enable the reader to gain a deeper understanding of self and others as well as encountering satisfying relationships among colleagues and students from a broad spectrum of perspectives. Most important, we will discuss how personal efficacy in this arena is empowering to both the faculty/staff person/administrator and the student. Last, we will talk about how small actions eventually build upon one another and can lead to transformational change (Gladwell, 2002; Keys, 1984).

We explore what it takes to inspire faculty, staff, and administrators to develop the courage and commitment to become builders. Not only builders who can take up the challenge of recognizing and responding to diversity flashpoint incidents, but builders willing to struggle and grow in the process of leading others through difficult interpersonal incidents based on identity difference. Builders can promote the importance of developing skills and attitudes to anticipate and respond to diversity flashpoints. These competencies will change faculty members' relationships with students and colleagues.

We discuss how diversity competencies may be recognized by selected peers and how this is likely to translate into becoming an informal mentor, advisor, and perhaps troubleshooter on difficult situations experienced by peers. We describe the attributes of effective mentoring (for example, Luna and Cullen, 1995) and how that ties into mentoring others to address diversity flashpoints in higher education.

The Leadership Challenge

Kouzes and Posner (1995, 2007) have developed well-researched practical and inspirational lessons for leaders in business, government, education, and community settings. Their "Five Practices of Exemplary Leadership" are based on studying people's peak leadership experiences to learn about competencies essential to getting astonishing things done in organizations. Although the stories differ, the research reveals five behavior patterns of leaders when they are at their personal best (www.leadershipchallenge.com): model the way, inspire a shared vision, challenge the process, enable others to act, and encourage the heart. In the next few pages, each behavior pattern is described, followed by how this might play out in the life of a diversity flashpoint mentor on a college campus.

Model the Way

Leaders establish principles for how people (constituents, peers, colleagues) should be treated and the way goals are pursued. They create standards of excellence and then set an example for others to follow, and they set short-term goals so that people can achieve small victories as they work toward larger objectives. They disentangle bureaucracy when it impedes action; they erect signposts when people are unsure of where to go or how to get there; and they create opportunities for victory.

To model the way, diversity flashpoint mentors on a college campus embrace the belief that bridging our differences forms our greatest strength as a campus community, and they commit to finding their way, publicly, onto the action continuum against oppression (see Chapter 6) in as many ways as possible. Flashpoint mentors are the people who respectfully intervene when someone makes a biased comment, when a student reports that a faculty member unintentionally shuts someone down in class, or when a staff member expresses frustration at hearing an unfamiliar language spoken in a departmental office.

Inspire a Shared Vision

Leaders are passionate that they can make a difference and can enlist others to help create a unique image of what the organization can become. They breathe life into their visions and get people excited about possibilities for the future. The diversity flashpoint mentor, though personally committed to recognizing and responding to students' identity differences, is able to capitalize on this personal commitment and attract others to the vision. He or she is the university professional who reaches out to others who are contemplating growing across difference, and helps them try out empowering, life changing behaviors aimed at fully engaging everyone in learning.

Challenge the Process

Leaders look for ways to change the status quo. They seek innovative ways to improve the organization by experimenting and taking risks. Because leaders know that this involves mistakes and failures, they accept mistakes not as failures but as learning opportunities. On a college campus, the diversity flashpoint mentor speaks up as an ally when a particular identity group is not represented in a high-stakes meeting, when a group is being characterized unfairly, when a search committee needs a little boost to screen candidates into a pool because of their identity differences, rather than screen them out because they look unfamiliar on paper.

Enable Others to Act

Leaders effect collaboration and build enthusiastic teams by actively involving others. They understand that mutual respect sustains extraordinary efforts. They strive to create an atmosphere of trust and human dignity. They strengthen others, enabling each person to feel capable and powerful. Diversity flashpoint mentors help committee members develop pride and strength in doing things differently, with different results. They are the ones to whom others look when teams are created and individual strengths are noted.

Encourage the Heart

Accomplishing extraordinary things in organizations is never easy. To sustain hope and determination, leaders recognize contributions of individuals and encourage group members to share in the rewards of their efforts. Leaders celebrate accomplishments and make people feel appreciated and valued. Indeed, diversity flashpoint mentors on university campuses are the people who, while they acknowledge the sheer energy it takes to make slight changes in the status quo, devote head, heart, and hands to making the campus climate better for everyone, no matter how long it takes.

Taken, together, these five behavior patterns (model the way, inspire a shared vision, challenge the process, enable others to act, and encourage the heart) can form a foundation for diversity flashpoint mentors to become builders, helping others experiment with supporting student identity differences.

Recruiting a Team in Support of Your Dream

Porras, Emery, and Thompson (2007) recount the story of Eleanor Josaitis, an outraged white woman who, after the 1967 Detroit race riots ended, moved her husband and five children from their comfortable middle class suburban home to the demographically black downtown. She founded "Focus: HOPE," a non-profit group aimed at ending racial tension. Today her organization brings together young, old, African American, and white, providing community arts programs, childcare, food programs, career training, and other outreach initiatives with 400 team members and 51,000 supporters. Eleanor Josaitis credits the team approach to the success of her organization:

> Anything worth doing can't be done alone. There's been too much hero worship about how just one person does it all.... You can make a difference.... It's about finding other people who get inspired by their own belief that they can make a difference in a similar way—you've got to find other leaders who can make it happen with you! (Porras et al., 2007, p. 202)

We're not all in this alone. Josaitis started with a team of committed relatives (her immediate family) and endured hate mail, firebombs, and relatives so angry with her life choices that they disowned her. Diversity flashpoint mentors may not experience direct threats to their lives, though they may be viewed with suspicion and skepticism by those committed to retaining the status quo. That is why it is critical to create alignment between what you are and what you do. It's about making that fit together.

We Make the Road by Walking

University professionals can begin the journey toward recognizing, reflecting on, and responding to diversity flashpoints in myriad ways. We are likely to view as cumbersome and uncomfortable the process of getting involved, being an ally, speaking up, or taking a stand when we witness (or initiate) a diversity flashpoint incident. This takes courage. However, if we believe that the educational process is inescapably defined by moral and political choices (Freire, 1970), we must follow our moral instinct and commit to taking small steps to halt oppression on university campuses.

Linking Faculty and Student Affairs Professionals

This book recognizes that although some professors may create a supportive environment conducive to student feedback, students tend to confide in campus professionals after a challenging interpersonal interaction with faculty (Garcia, Hoelscher, and Farmer, 2005). This points to the potential value of faculty, staff, and administrators who work together across institutional boundaries effectively to manage diversity flashpoint situations involving students.

Given the typical power differential between faculty and students (especially when a course grade is involved or a letter of reference hangs in the balance), open and honest interpersonal feedback often proves difficult for students. Two ideas to address this challenge surfaced during our initial research, and have continued to guide the development of our thinking in this book.

First, the importance of building alliances. Through our research we heard repeatedly that student affairs professionals are interested in working with faculty and staff members to better support university students. Faculty and staff may find that alliances with campus professionals who work regularly as problem-solvers on behalf of students will enhance their ability to recognize and reflect on diversity flashpoints. With the benefit of this information, faculty and staff can develop effective responses to these situations.

Second, the importance of sharing information. Student affairs professionals with expertise in teaching and learning may help uncover classroom strategies for providing growth-oriented feedback to faculty members who unintentionally step into a potentially hurtful diversity flashpoint situation. The policy implication of this work is to systematically create information flow between academic leadership professionals and faculty and staff aimed at enhancing the learning environment for all students, especially those whose identity differences are most unlike our own.

In their synthesis of empirical evidence about the benefits of student diversity, Milem, Chang, and Antonio (2005) urge campus leaders to realize and implement three principles of practice: (1) take a multidimensional approach (i.e., one size does not fit all); (2) engage all students (i.e., encourage "border crossing" by all); and (3) focus on process (i.e., view diversity as a means toward achieving educational outcomes, versus being an end in itself). These principles underscore our firmly held belief: engaging diversity to improve students' lives on campus must involve myriad strategies that are constantly changing to benefit various groups, and university campuses are dynamic communities that are works in progress.

Epilogue

Think back to Chapter 5, which opened with a vignette describing two university students being prejudged by university staff members for speaking in their native Vietnamese language in an office area. The staff members wonder out loud, "Don't they know they are in America and going to an American university to get educated?"

The room suddenly grew quiet and all eyes turned to you. You noticed the pained looks on the students' faces, and the questioning looks on the faces of the staff members who were involved in the negative comments.

What *could* you say and do to support everyone involved in this diversity flashpoint? There are myriad responses, from low-stake to higher-stake responses. What are the options for action?

What *should* you do? Given the options you've brainstormed above, what outcomes might occur for each type of action, and how do you think each of the players might respond?

What *will* you do? There's the big question. One of these options surfaces as the one most likely to lead to the most positive outcome for everyone. You know which one it is. Take a breath, step forward, and do it.

Finally, how is this incident, and any other like it, reported throughout the university? What structures and processes exist to enable everyone to learn from the incident and take the necessary steps to enable everyone to make the campus a better learning environment for all?

REFERENCES

Ambrosio, J. (2003). We make the road by walking. In G. Gay (Ed.), *Becoming multicultural educators: Personal journey toward professional agency* (pp. 17–41). San Francisco: Jossey-Bass.

American Council on Education. (2006). *89th Annual Meeting.* Retrieved February 23, 2007, from http://www.aceannualmeeting.org/about_ace.cfm.

Bergin, T. G. (Ed.). (1947). Machiavelli: The Prince. New York: Appleton Century Crofts.

Freire, P. (1970). *Pedagogy of the oppressed.* New York: Continuum.

Garcia, J. E., Hoelscher, K. J., and Farmer, V. L. (2005). Diversity flashpoints: Understanding difficult interpersonal situations grounded in identity difference. *Innovative Higher Education,* 29(4), 275–289.

Gladwell, M. (2002). *The tipping point: How little things can make a big difference.* Boston: Little Brown.

Keys, Jr., K. (1984). *The hundredth monkey* (2nd ed.). Marina Del Ray: DeVorss & Co.

Kouzes, J. M., and Posner, B. Z. (1995). *The leadership challenge: How to keep getting extraordinary things done in organizations.* San Francisco: Jossey-Bass.

Kouzes, J. M., and Posner, B. Z. (2007). *The leadership challenge: How to keep getting extraordinary things done in organizations.* Retrieved April 29, 2007, from www.leadershipchallenge.com.

Locke, E. A., Latham, G. P., and Erez, M. (1988). The determinants of goal commitment. *Academy of Management Review,* 13(1), 23–39.

Luft, J., and Ingham, H. (1955). The Johari window: A graphic model of interpersonal awareness. *Proceedings of the Western Training Laboratory in Group Development.* Los Angeles: UCLA.

Luna, G., and Cullen, D. (1995). *Empowering the faculty: Mentoring redirected and renewed.* Washington DC: George Washington University, Graduate School of Education and Human Development. (ERIC Clearinghouse on Higher Education, ED399888.)

Milem, J. F., Chang, M. J., and Antonio, A. L. (2005). Making diversity work on campus. In the *Making excellence inclusive initiative: Preparing students and campuses for an era of greater expectations.* Washington, DC: American Association of Colleges and Universities (AAC&U). [Electronic version]. http://siher.stanford.edu/AntonioMilemChang_makingdiversitywork.pdf.

Porras, J., Emery, S., and Thompson, M. (2007). *Success built to last: Creating a life that matters.* Upper Saddle River: Pearson Education.

Raines, C., and Ewing, L. (2006). *The art of connecting: How to overcome differences, build rapport, and communicate effectively with anyone.* Upper Saddle River: Pearson Education.

Streckel, R., and Streckel, M. (n.d.). *The Milestone Project.* Retrieved April 29, 2007, from http://milestonesproject.com/index.php/big_picture.

Taflinger, R. (n.d.). "Taking Advantage." www.wsu.edu:8080/~taflinge/index.html.

APPENDICES:
Workshop Materials

APPENDIX A: TEMPLATE FOR A PROFESSIONAL
DEVELOPMENT WORKSHOP FOR FACULTY AND STAFF
(120 minutes, including a 15-minute break)

Objective: To assist faculty and staff development aimed at identifying and practicing strategies for responding effectively to difficult interpersonal situations with students related to cultural identity differences.

Rationale: Because of demographic changes and societal expectations, there is increasing pressure for faculty and others in higher education to effectively manage identity differences. Through this workshop we are attempting to build greater competencies among higher education professionals, and as a result modeling for others (students, co-workers) ways to become more effective professionals in diverse communities.

Definition: A *diversity flashpoint incident* is a difficult interpersonal situation during a faculty or staff interaction with a student (or students) that originates from an area of identity difference (e.g., race, class, gender, ethnicity, sexual orientation, language, religion, ability/disability). These incidents can have either positive or negative outcomes, and are described by students as ranging from less significant (isolated events or less hurtful situations) to very significant (repeated events or singularly devastating behaviors causing students to withdraw from college). A flashpoint incident results in some or all people present feeling there has been a broken connection between people who should be working together on a common task—teaching and learning. Troubling to most is that the broken connection is linked to membership in a group and brings up the specter of an "-ism" in operation (e.g., racism, sexism etc.).

Orientation: Our research demonstrates that diversity flashpoint incidents occur in the lives of faculty, staff, and students across a wide range of colleges and universities. Although these incidents tend to cluster around a relatively small set of settings and issues, these situations have the potential to adversely impact student learning and effective teaching. While higher education professionals may have completed mandated training in topics such as sexual harassment, few are trained to expand their intercultural sensitivity.

This lack of preparedness creates more challenges as educators aspire to enable their students to become better prepared to live in a more diverse and global rather than parochial world. Left unaddressed, the inability to effectively address diversity flashpoints may continue to contribute to students' disillusionment with their place on college campuses and discourage faculty and staff from engaging with students whose cultural attributes are different from theirs.

APPENDIX B: WORKSHOP GOALS

1. Engage participants' emotional and intellectual attention using *local* diversity flashpoint stories collected prior to the workshop;

2. Facilitate participants' consideration of critical issues and potential effective responses to a set of *national* diversity flashpoint stories representative of the core settings and issues uncovered by our research;

3. Guide participants' *skill development* using a variety of research-based strategies supportive of individuals involved in various flashpoint incidents; and

4. Focus participants' attention on *tangible, actionable outcomes* related to college mission (e.g., training thoughtful, knowledgeable, effective professionals for a diverse society) and achieving standards of excellence in teacher preparation (such as, NCATE Standard 4: Diversity; Standard 5: Faculty Qualifications, Performance and Development).

Pre-Session Assignment for Workshop Participants

A week or so before the workshop, invite participants to bring a personally relevant diversity flashpoint to the workshop. Have them complete the "Diversity Flashpoint Form" (Appendix C) to describe a story that meets the characteristics of a diversity flashpoint, including what happened, how it was handled, and the results. Bring extras on the day of the workshop for those who will complete it as the workshop begins.

Pre-Session Assignment for Small Group Leaders

A few days before the workshop, gather together and train a small group of colleagues to act as discussion leaders for the small group activity. Use the "Group Leader Notes for Supporting Small Group Discussion" handout (Appendix D) to familiarize them with the 4 R's approach to developing mindful skills for recognizing, reflecting, and responding in diversity flashpoint situations.

Workshop Session

I. Introductions, Overview, Ground Rules (10 minutes)

- Welcome, thanks for coming, introductions;
- Overview: Today's professional development session is designed to help you discover ways to recognize and respond to difficult interpersonal

situations with others that originate from areas of identity difference (e.g., race, class, gender, ethnicity, sexual orientation, language, religion, ability, or disability);

• During the next few hours you will share and hear about some local diversity flashpoints, work with some nationally-collected flashpoints, practice responding to situations like the one you brought to share today, and provide feedback about your experience today and next steps that would guide your learning in this area.

• Some ground rules for discussion:

  • Listen for understanding,
  • Respect multiple points of view,
  • Explore assumptions and reasoning behind positions or viewpoints,
  • Own our feelings and prescriptions, and
  • Strive to make the learning space safe for all.

II. History—Western Washington University Diversity Flashpoint Project (i.e., Talking Points for Setting the Context of the Workshop) (5 minutes)

• Handout 1: Diversity Flashpoints Research Foundations, Methods, Results, and Implications for Practice and Policy (Appendix E)

III. Sharing Local Incidents (i.e., Thawing Old Attitudes) (15 minutes)

• Handout 2: Guidelines for Small Group Discussion of Diversity Flash-point Situations and Some Ground Rules for Discussion (Appendix F)

• Form small groups of 4–6 individuals, each with a trained leader who reminds participants of ground rules for discussion;

• In each subgroup, individuals share the incident they either experienced or observed;

• Group identifies themes that run through the collected incidents; and

• Subgroup leader shares key points from one story and/or a theme with the entire group of participants.

IV. Overview of Strategies for Working with Research-Based Diversity Flashpoint Vignettes (10 minutes)

• Review the 4 R's process: recognize, reflect, respond, reassess ("A Model for Managing Diversity Flashpoint Incidents");

• Review the continuum of potential responses to a diversity flashpoint incident ("Action Continuum for Interrupting Oppressive Behavior");

- Review the goal of enabling participants to develop a more sophisticated awareness of multiple strategies to address diversity flashpoint incidents (i.e., rather than thinking narrowly about one right way to handle a challenging situation, consider a range of appropriate responses to support those involved);
- Reinforce the notion that enhancing one's ability as an educator is a journey of personal learning as well as continual improvement as a scholar and expert in one's area of expertise;
- Provide a framework for understanding the nature of the vignette analysis questions including imagining different organizational contexts for each vignette (e.g., hostile diversity climate versus welcoming diversity climate) and how that might inform which paths of action might be more successful; and
- Assign Vignette #1 for everyone to read and reflect upon individually.

BREAK: 15 minutes; on return assemble in original small groups of 5 or fewer.

V. Developing Strategies for Addressing Diversity Flashpoint Vignettes (i.e., Developing New Attitudes and Skills) (30 minutes)

- Engage each subgroup in a discussion of Vignette #1 with these objectives:
  - Understand the issue and setting,
  - Appreciate the impacts organizational context might have on possible responses to the incident,
  - Investigate potential strategies for addressing the incident,
  - Discuss lessons learned from the analysis of the vignette, and
  - Share key points and lessons learned from studying and interacting with the vignette;
- Repeat this process with Vignette #2, building skills and strategies from previous round of analysis and enactments;
- Engage groups in sharing their strategies; and
- Transition, returning to local diversity flashpoint incidents.

VI. Applying Diversity Flashpoint Competencies to a Local Incident (i.e., Consolidating Learning by Applying the 4 R's Method to a Local Flashpoint Story) (15 minutes)

- In subgroups, trios of individuals revisit one of the local incidents they brought to the workshop to further analyze and develop potential appropriate strategies for effective action;

- Trios enact a mini-role play where each person practices a strategy to address the incident and the next person builds on it. This leads to group capacity building versus putting one person on the spot:
  - Both role players read the incident,
  - "Person in charge" gets coaching from third person, (who could also act as an additional person in the incident as needed),
  - Role play the incident using the 4 R's,
  - Debrief, and
  - Switch roles so each person gets to be person in charge;
- Share lessons learned from addressing the local incident;
- What themes evolved? What did you learn?

VII. Synthesis (i.e., Time for Lingering Questions, Personal Meaning-Making, and Deeply Embedded Concerns) (15 minutes)

- Re-convene in three (or more) discussion groups based on participants' professional assignments and/or interests and:
  - Discuss how participants might take the knowledge, skills, and dispositions into their everyday work lives as professionals,
  - Report back to large group a few ideas about how participants might use these ideas and strategies, and
  - What did you find meaningful, memorable about today's activities?

VIII. Workshop Evaluation (5 minutes)

- Handout 3: Feedback Form, Diversity Flashpoints Professional Development Workshop (Appendix G)
- What support do you need to better address identity differences of students on our campus? How might you generate this support?
- What ideas or techniques did you learn in this session that might help you on your job?
- What do you wish we had covered or spent more time on?
- Ideas for future workshops?

APPENDIX C: DIVERSITY FLASHPOINT FORM

A diversity flashpoint incident is a potentially explosive interpersonal situation between faculty/staff and students that arises out of identity difference. We define identity differences inclusively to refer to the constellation of characteristics that connect us to a social reference group (e.g., race, class, gender, ethnicity, language, sexual orientation, age, size, family structure, ability/disability). A diversity flashpoint incident results in some or all people present feeling like there has been a broken connection between people who should be working together on a common task: teaching and learning. Troubling to most is that the broken connection is linked to membership in a group and brings up the specter of an "-ism" in operation (e.g., racism, sexism, etc.).

Here are some examples of diversity flashpoint situations:

- A Native American student angrily points out during one of your lectures that she is concerned about the coverage of typical developmental patterns of Native American preschoolers;

- Two staff members, in the presence of students speaking a language other than English, discuss their view that everyone should be speaking English on campus;

- You overhear two students talking as you walk toward your office about someone "acting so gay" or referring to something as "so retarded"; and

- You hear an African American student complain to another student about how she is frequently asked in class to give the African American perspective on issues by her instructors.

In the box below, briefly describe a "flashpoint-like" situation you have observed or been part of. Be general in your description; do not mention people's names. Focus on what happened, how it was handled, and the results.

What happened? (i.e., Describe the diversity flashpoint situation, from your point of view.)	How was it handled? (i.e., What did people do?)	What were the results? (i.e., If positive, what accounted for this? If negative, can you think of how it might have been handled differently?)

In thinking about this event ask yourself to recognize, reflect, and respond to the incident.

Recognize:
Reflect (in your own mind):
Respond:

APPENDIX D: GROUP LEADER NOTES FOR SUPPORTING SMALL GROUP DISCUSSION

Diversity Flashpoints Workshop

One aspect of effective teaching is the ability to reflect on practice (Schon, 1987, 1991). Reflection on action can occur vicariously through reading and discussion of authentic teaching cases. The suggestions below attempt to create a scaffold for participants at your table to reflect on a case. This is not to suggest a linear process must be systematically followed to "crack the case," but that effective problem-solvers consider several ideas simultaneously and revisit others recursively. Similarly, there are considerations in the scaffold that participants will omit and others on which they will spend considerable time.

A Three-Step Approach to Discussing a Flashpoint Situation:

I. Recognize the Problem. A reflective practitioner starts by recognizing that there is a problem or a discrepancy between what one expects and what is actually occurring.

To help participants recognize the problem:

- Urge them to identify what is happening between characters in the case and to describe the discrepancy between their expectations and what has occurred.
- Remind them to stick to the facts presented in the case without making interpretations regarding beliefs, motivation, and actions.

II. Reflect on the Problem. People frame problems on the basis of their own values, experiences, and assumptions. While participants may be in agreement about the facts in a case, they may disagree on the issues involved and how to resolve them ethically and equitably.

To help participants frame the problem:

- Encourage them to consider the problem from multiple perspectives.
- Encourage them to listen to others do the same.

III. Respond with Alternatives. The experiences and expertise of people from different backgrounds (faculty, staff, and administrators) are particularly valuable when searching for alternative plans of action.

To help participants search for alternatives:

- Challenge participants to generate a list of alternatives.
- Encourage them to examine the short- and long-term consequences of each decision for all stakeholders.

Help participants decide which alternatives seem acceptable, given the needs of stakeholders.

APPENDIX E: HANDOUT 1–DIVERSITY FLASHPOINTS RESEARCH FOUNDATIONS, METHODS, RESULTS, AND IMPLICATIONS FOR PRACTICE AND POLICY

Research Foundations, Methods, Results

- Research aimed at exploring the topography of difficult diversity situations among faculty, staff, and students in educational settings;
- Qualitative study based on interviews of 34 student affairs professionals from 11 U.S. universities (2001–2004);
- Uncovered 153 usable incidents and classified incidents by issues and settings; and
- Published findings: Innovative Higher Education, 29 (4), 2005.

Flashpoint Incident Characteristics

Settings refers to the type of behavioral situation where the incident occurred:

- Expectations for Learning (structure or process used to set student learning expectations),
- Curriculum and Content (course content and its relationship to diversity issues),
- Learning Management (managing the interactive process between students and faculty/staff), and
- Assessment (methods and requirements associated with assessing learning).

Issues refers to the identity-based diversity issue that creates a challenging interpersonal experience:

- Support Special Students,
- Treatment of a Lone Member of an Underrepresented Group,
- Treatment of Non-Native English Speakers,
- Interacting with Individuals Who Are Different,
- Using Terms That Label Others in Ways That Devalue,
- Responding as an Ally,
- Recognizing and Valuing, and
- Addressing the Use of Coercive Power.

Research Findings and Implications

- Developed flashpoint settings and issues framework,
- Recognized that flashpoint incidents tend to cluster in certain settings and on particular issues,
- Recognized that school type and mission are related respectively to issues and settings,
- Results suggest that faculty and staff development in diversity should be targeted to flashpoint-rich situations,
- Results represent multiple schools and school specific research could be used to design locally valid faculty development curriculum, and
- Suggest follow-up research to validate these findings and understand why issues cluster in certain settings.

APPENDIX F: HANDOUT 2—GUIDELINES FOR SMALL GROUP DISCUSSION OF DIVERSITY FLASHPOINT SITUATIONS AND SOME GROUND RULES FOR DISCUSSION

Use this three-step approach to developing mindful skills for addressing future unexpected diversity flashpoints that will find their way into our professional lives.

1. **Recognize**
   DESCRIBE what is happening between the characters in this vignette, and remember to stick to the facts.

2. **Reflect**
   EXPLORE the situation from multiple perspectives including from the point of view of the characters in the vignette, the participants in your group, and academic theory.

3. **Respond**
   DETERMINE alternative approaches to addressing the situation described in the vignette, weighing both short- and long-term consequences of these actions for the stakeholders involved.

Some Ground Rules for Discussion

- Listen for understanding.
- Respect multiple points of view.
- Explore assumptions and reasoning behind positions or viewpoints.
- Own our feelings and prescriptions.
- Strive to make the learning space safe for all.

APPENDIX G: HANDOUT 3—FEEDBACK FORM, DIVERSITY FLASHPOINTS PROFESSIONAL DEVELOPMENT WORKSHOP

Supporting your growth in recognizing and responding to student identity differences

1. What kinds of support do you need to better address the identity differences of students in our college and on our campus?

2. How might you access or generate this support?

3. What ideas or techniques did you learn about in this session that might help you on your job?

4. In the overall context of our workshop, what might we have missed, or what do you wish we had covered/spent more time on?

5. Any other thoughts you care to share? Ideas for future workshops?

APPENDIX H: COLLECTION OF TWENTY-FOUR DIVERSITY FLASHPOINT VIGNETTES

Vignette #1: What Is a Family?

I. SYNOPSIS

For the past 15 years, Dr. Terry Rusk has taught the popular Sociology of the Family course at a private, religiously affiliated university located in the Midwest. Though a main focus of the course is the structure of the family, Dr. Rusk does not typically include issues facing gay or lesbian families. During one course session covering family structures, a student describes the experience of growing up with two mothers. Some students begin to giggle. Others laugh nervously. Professor Rusk continues lecturing. The student who spoke out glares at the class and demands, "What are you laughing at?" Professor Rusk begins lecturing again as if nothing has happened.

II. TEACHING NOTES: WHAT IS A FAMILY?

Introduction

The purpose of this teaching Vignette is to consider the role of the faculty member in supporting students in being able to engage on free inquiry without derision. The Vignette shows how both teachers and students struggle to respect differences in family structures in the context of historic views of what is proper family structure.

The Vignette also challenges the faculty member in terms of questioning what topics should be in the curriculum. An analysis of the role of the faculty member, an expert, versus scholar-learner can provide useful discussion about the eventual outcome of the situation.

Discussion Questions

1. What is happening in this case? What surprised you in this case? Why?

2. How do the central issues relate to issues you've faced?

3. Why do you think the students began to laugh? To what extent do you believe the student's response to classmates will help open more fruitful dialog around family structure? What are the pros and cons for the student who spoke up? How likely is it that there is another student in the class who understands and has empathy for the student's view and experience? Why do you hold these opinions?

4. What should Professor Rusk do in this situation? Assuming something will be done, when should Professor Rusk act?

5. What assumptions do you think the rest of the class make about the student with the question? Why?

6. What are your thoughts about how Professor Rusk chooses to respond?

7. What institutional conditions might support addressing this situation in a productive manner? What conditions might hinder a supportive response?

8. What situations have you encountered that resemble this one? How did you respond? Given your experience, what would you do now?

Vignette #2: The Xenophobic Comment

I. SYNOPSIS

Pat Johnson, a faculty member at a regional university in the Pacific Northwest, stops by her departmental office to pick up mail. On her way into the office she notices two students waiting to talk with the receptionist. The students, first-generation Americans, are conversing animatedly in Vietnamese while they wait to be helped. Dr. Johnson hears the administrative assistant say to the receptionist, "I don't know why these students speak to one another in that foreign language! Don't they know they are in America and going to an American University to get educated?" The room suddenly becomes quiet. Pat quickly turns and notices the pained looks on the students' faces. The receptionist looks questioningly up at Pat.

II. TEACHING NOTES: THE XENOPHOBIC COMMENT

Introduction

The purpose of this teaching Vignette is to consider the role of the faculty member in supporting students. The Vignette shows how both teachers and staff members struggle to balance personal freedoms with respectful language.

The Vignette is designed to focus on issues of student support, but can also be used to discuss issues of student–student communication, staff–staff communication, and faculty members' involvement in students' learning outside of the classroom.

An analysis using principles of personal empowerment and student support is especially applicable to this teaching case.

Discussion Questions

1. What is happening in this case? What surprised you in this case?

2. How do the central issues relate to issues you've faced?

3. Why do you think the administrative assistant made the comment to the receptionist? What are the pros and cons of speaking up for Pat?

4. To what extent do you think the faculty member should take responsibility for the remarks of a departmental staff member, such as their views about language used by students?

5. What assumptions does Pat make about the administrative assistant? About the receptionist? About the students? How can Pat learn more about these beliefs?

6. What are your thoughts about how Pat chooses to intervene? How Pat communicates with the administrative assistant and receptionist? How Pat communicates with the students?

7. What role should Pat play in supporting students in such situations? What are some ways Pat could mobilize the university's resources to address similar situations?

8. What institutional conditions might support addressing this situation in a productive manner? What conditions might hinder a supportive response?

9. What situations have you encountered that resemble this one? How did you respond? Given your experience, what would you do now?

Vignette #3: When Collaboration and Cheating Meet

I. SYNOPSIS

Several first-generation Asian American students are peers in a computer science course. They approach the instructor for clarification about a particularly challenging out-of-class assignment. The faculty member, Dr. Terry O'Brien, refuses to unpack his thinking about the assignment, urging them to "just do your best." The students discuss the assignment together and subsequently develop and hand in individual responses to the assignment. Dr. O'Brien is surprised at the similarity in the responses of this group of students to the assignment. He immediately sets up a meeting with the students to discuss the cheating policy on campus. Nervously, he phones you, his mentor, to discuss the issue with him before the meeting.

II. TEACHING NOTES: WHEN COLLABORATION AND CHEATING MEET

Introduction

The purpose of this teaching Vignette is to consider the role of the faculty member in supporting students. The Vignette shows how both teachers and staff members struggle to balance expectations about completing course assignments with students' cultural beliefs about working together.

The Vignette is designed to focus on issues of student support, but can also be used to discuss issues of student–faculty communication, faculty–faculty communication, and faculty members' involvement in students' learning outside of the classroom.

An analysis using principles of student support and faculty mentoring is especially applicable to this teaching case.

Discussion Questions

1. What is happening in this case? What surprised you in this case?
2. How do the central issues relate to issues you've faced?
3. Why do you think the problem occurred? What are the pros and cons of accusing students of cheating? What are the alternatives?
4. To what extent do you think the instructor should take responsibility for the approach students took to developing their responses?
5. What assumptions does the instructor make about the students? How can he learn more about these beliefs?
6. What are your thoughts about inviting a mentor to intervene? What do you think about how the instructor communicates with his mentor?
7. What role should the instructor's mentor play in supporting his colleague in such situations? What are some ways the mentor could mobilize the university's resources to address similar situations?
8. What institutional conditions might support addressing this situation in a productive manner? What conditions might hinder a supportive response?
9. What situations have you encountered that resemble this one? How did you respond? Given your experience, what would you do now?

Vignette #4: The Challenge

I. SYNOPSIS

Chris Williams, a faculty member in teacher education, welcomes her new students on the first day of class. During the first several class sessions, the lone student of color in the class (a Native American female) makes increasingly strong statements that challenge the way the way the instructor characterizes non-White children, especially those of Native American heritage. Dr. Williams hears the statements and asks the student to hold them for later. Frustrated, the student leaves class and storms into the office of the department chair to request a formal meeting with the instructor present.

II. TEACHING NOTES: THE CHALLENGE

Introduction

The purpose of this teaching Vignette is to consider the role of the faculty member in supporting open and honest classroom dialogue. The Vignette shows how both teachers and students struggle to balance the presentation of course content and the expression of student opinion.

The Vignette is designed to focus on issues of student support, but can also be used to discuss issues of student-student communication, staff-staff communication, and faculty members' involvement in creating supportive classroom environments.

An analysis using principles of positive communication and student support is especially applicable to this teaching case.

Discussion Questions

1. What is happening in this case? What surprised you in this case?

2. How do the central issues relate to issues you've faced?

3. Why do you think the student felt she must assert her opinion in class? Why do you think the instructor delayed a response to the assertions of the student? What are the pros and cons of speaking up for the student? What are the alternatives? What are the pros and cons of addressing immediately the student concern for the instructor?

4. To what extent do you think the instructor should take responsibility for the action of the student after she left the classroom?

5. What assumptions does the student make about the instructor? About the department chair? About her student peers in the class? How can the instructor learn more about these beliefs?

6. What are your thoughts about how the department chair should intervene? How the department chair communicates with the student?

7. What role should the instructor play in supporting students in such situations? What are some ways the instructor could mobilize the university's resources to address similar situations?

8. What institutional conditions might support addressing this situation in a productive manner? What conditions might hinder a supportive response?

9. What situations have you encountered that resemble this one? How did you respond? Given your experience, what would you do now?

Vignette #5: A Case of Appropriation

I. SYNOPSIS

A committee of twelve, composed of faculty, staff, and students, are gathered in a meeting to discuss issues related to curriculum design and student retention. Early in the meeting, one of the two student representatives (and the only person of color at the meeting) proposes an approach that takes into consideration the impact of race and socioeconomic class to addressing the issues at hand. The conversation around the table briefly acknowledges the contribution and moves on to other issues. Later in the discussion a senior member of the committee proposes the same approach to addressing the issue. Immediately, the group agrees with the idea. The senior member gives the proposal a name and the group then refers to the named proposal as his/hers. The student looks left and right, then stares down at the table and withdraws from the conversation. You begin to notice some dissonance in the group process.

II. TEACHING NOTES: A CASE OF APPROPRIATION

Introduction

The purpose of this teaching Vignette is to consider the role of members of teams and workgroups to acknowledge the contributions of all team members to the work of the whole. The Vignette shows how more powerful individuals command the attention of others and gain unearned privilege by appropriating the contributions of group members who are less powerful.

The Vignette is designed to draw attention to the notion that the assignment of authorship is the responsibility of the community and reflects on the integrity of the group and the ability of the group to sustain member participation.

An analysis using the notion of diffusion of responsibility and lack of agency among group members to manage privilege equitably will generate productive discussion.

Discussion Questions

1. What is happening in this case? What surprised you in this case?
2. How do the central issues relate to issues you've faced?
3. How do you think the student felt when his/her contribution was politely acknowledged but not taken up?
4. Why do you think that no one mentioned that the idea was originated by the student?

5. What are the pros and cons of speaking up for the student? Whose responsibility is it, if anyone's, to speak up? What are the alternatives?

6. What assumptions can you make about the senior person? Why?

7. What institutional conditions might support addressing this situation in a productive manner? What conditions might hinder a supportive response?

8. What situations have you encountered that resemble this one? How did you respond? Given your experience, what would you do now?

Vignette #6: If It Is Not from Here It Must Not Be Good?

I. SYNOPSIS

Kamala Lahiri is a student from India studying to obtain her education degree. For class, students were required to read a chapter from their textbook about effective use of instructional technology. In class discussion the next day, Kamala raised her hand, and when the professor called on her, she said, "I feel that the information in the chapter we read last night was really dated. In fact, I noticed that this book was published three years ago, and I think some of what it says is not state-of-the-art." The instructor responded, "You mean you people read books like this in your country?"

II. TEACHING NOTES: IF IT IS NOT FROM HERE IT MUST NOT BE GOOD?

Introduction

The purpose of this teaching Vignette is to consider the role of the faculty member in supporting open and honest classroom dialogue. The Vignette shows how the use of language can marginalize students and create a climate that hinders learning and development.

In addition to the focusing on opportunities for dialogue, this Vignette can be used to foster a discussion of how faculty respond to challenges in the classroom and how attitudes about the credibility of "foreign"-based information is perceived and addressed.

An analysis of how roles and person characteristics (i.e., nationality, status) can impact the way challenging questions are addressed is applicable to this Vignette.

Discussion Questions

1. What is happening in this case? What surprised you in this case?

2. How do the central issues relate to issues you've faced?

3. Why do you think the student felt she must assert her opinion in class? What assumptions does the student make about the instructor?

4. Why do you think the instructor responded the way he/she did? What assumptions did he/she make about the student?

5. What are the pros and cons of speaking up for the student? What are the alternatives?

6. What, if anything, should the other students do in this situation? Why?

7. What institutional conditions might support addressing this situation in a productive manner? What conditions might hinder a supportive response?

8. What situations have you encountered that resemble this one? How did you respond? Given your experience, what would you do now?

Vignette #7: Bending over Backwards?

I. SYNOPSIS

Kerry Jenkins, a white instructor, teaches introductory management in a small private university. During office hours, Alex Martinez, a first-year Hispanic student, comes and admits to having some trouble understanding the concepts from the lecture. Kerry, wanting to do the right thing for a minority student, spends an hour explaining terms and definitions to the student. During the following weeks, Kerry sees Alex during office hours, explaining and re-explaining the lectures. After the first exam, Kerry is disappointed to see that Alex has only earned a C. The next time Alex comes to office hours, Kerry complains, "I am really upset with you, Alex. I bent over backwards for you, and you really let me down."

II. TEACHING NOTES: BENDING OVER BACKWARDS?

Introduction

The purpose of this teaching Vignette is to illustrate the challenges that face instructors in attempting to help students and in acknowledging their own struggles around ownership of student challenges, especially for students of color.

This Vignette offers an opportunity to explore the complexity associated with the performance of students from "at-risk" populations. It also brings to light questions about how an instructor's sense of satisfaction is associated with their expectations of students.

Discussion Questions

1. What is happening in this case? What surprised you in this case?

2. How do the central issues relate to issues you've faced?

3. Who is really "benefiting" from the meetings during office hours?

4. What assumptions is the instructor making about the student?

5. Does Alex have a viable choice about how to use his time? Why? Why not?

6. What assumptions do you think the student is making about the instructor? How does this affect his actions?

7. What role should the instructor play in supporting students in such situations?

8. What institutional conditions might support addressing this situation in a productive manner? What conditions might hinder a supportive response?

9. What situations have you encountered that resemble this one? How did you respond? Given your experience, what would you do now?

Vignette #8: The Resumé

I. SYNOPSIS

Chris Pozos is a senior majoring in electrical engineering. Chris is a good student, is very personable, and has the talents to become an excellent engineer. During Chris's undergraduate career, he has been involved in a number of leadership positions in the university's Lesbian/Bisexual/Gay/Transgender Alliance (LGBTA). Chris has been successful in providing leadership in student programming and improving the climate around issues of sexual orientation on campus and especially in the college of engineering.

Terry Bishop is Chris's faculty advisor. Chris has been in several of Terry's courses and done well. During a scheduled appointment, Terry and Chris discuss what Chris wants to do after graduation. Towards the end of a healthy conversation, Chris asks Terry for advice on what to include in a strong resume. Of concern for Chris is what to do about including involvement in LBGTA activities. Chris shares that these activities indicate a record of successful leadership and the placement center's materials say that sort of evidence is important in getting a job. Terry's first thought is that this is a very difficult question to answer.

II. TEACHING NOTES: THE RESUMÉ

Introduction

The purpose of this Vignette is to consider the role of the faculty member in helping students make informed decisions that support the student as a person.

The Vignette is designed to focus on faculty–student communication and student support. It also aims to stimulate examination about assumptions and stereotypes held about the individuals portrayed in the Vignette as well as the academic discipline and job market.

An analysis of attributional biases is applicable to this case. A discussion of the skills faculty need to effectively address this issue would also be useful.

Discussion Questions

1. What is happening in this case? How would you describe the critical issues in the case?

2. What was your first reaction to this situation? Why did you have this reaction?

3. What assumptions did you make about Chris, Terry, the field of Engineering, and the Job Market?

4. What alternative actions might Terry take? What are the consequences of these actions for Terry and Chris?

5. What course of action would you take if you were Terry? Why?

6. If you had to recommend how to handle this situation to another faculty member, what would you say?

7. What institutional conditions might support addressing this situation in a productive manner? What conditions might hinder a supportive response?

8. What situations have you encountered that resemble this one? How did you respond? Given your experience, what would you do now?

Vignette #9: Being the Only One and Being Misidentified

I. SYNOPSIS

Emanuel Jimenez is a member of one of the student clubs in the college of business at his university. Emanuel is one of the few students in the club who is not White. The club is quite active and frequently brings in outside speakers to talk to students about current issues in business and economics. The most recent panel of speakers has addressed issues related to the changes in the labor market, globalization, immigration, the flow of labor around the world, and the impact on U.S.-based firms.

At a club meeting, one of the student officers points to Emanuel and says, "Hey, Emanuel, what do you people think about all this illegal alien stuff. You know, we Americans think it is unfair that illegals take away jobs from citizens who deserve those jobs."

Emanuel, who happens to be of Puerto Rican ancestry, looks down, and quietly says, "Everyone deserves a chance" before he gets up and leaves the room. The faculty advisor looks up and sees everyone else quite puzzled at the interaction.

II. TEACHING NOTES: BEING THE ONLY ONE AND BEING MISIDENTIFIED.

Introduction

The purpose of this Vignette is to consider the role of the faculty member in recognizing the impact of lack of numeric diversity in the dynamics of discussion and inquiry. The Vignette portrays a situation that challenges the advisor to take action in a caring and assertive fashion.

This Vignette also provides an opportunity to explore the diversity that exists within minority groups (e.g., Puerto Ricans, Cubans, Mexicans, etc.) and how the specific ethnic context plays a role in the conversation.

Discussion Questions

1. What is happening in this case? What surprised you in this case? Why?
2. How do the central issues relate to issues you've faced?
3. Why do you think the student club officer asked Emmanuel the question?
4. What assumptions do you think the student had about Emmanuel?
5. While he chose not to speak up, what are the pros and cons for Emmanuel in speaking up? How likely is it that there is another student in the class who understands and has empathy for his view and experience?
6. What should the faculty advisor do in this situation? Assuming something will be done, when should the advisor act?

7. What assumptions do you think the rest of the students make about the student club officer with the question? Why?

8. What institutional conditions might support addressing this situation in a productive manner? What conditions might hinder a supportive response?

9. What situations have you encountered that resemble this one? How did you respond? Given your experience, what would you do now?

Vignette #10: Privilege Can Blind

I. SYNOPSIS

During a discussion of the history of civil rights in an American Cultural Studies class, several students get into a heated discussion about the impact of slavery on families. June, an African American student, reacts by saying, "You don't understand, my family lives with the legacy of our family being broken up against their own will. We don't have your privileged experience of having a traceable family tree." Bill, a student in the class, responds by saying, "June, that is all in the past so we might as well move on. Lighten up." June glares at Bill and the professor decides to intervene sensing that the discussion is about to get out of control.

II. TEACHING NOTES: PRIVILEGE CAN BLIND

Introduction

The purpose of this Vignette is to consider the role of the faculty member in helping students recognize and appreciate differences in experience.

An analysis of the unspoken dialogue can provide a discussion of the hidden assumptions that are held in cross-race interactions. The Vignette offers an opportunity for a discussion of effective conflict management skills and how those skills could be applied in creating open dialogue.

Discussion Questions

1. What is happening in this case? What surprised you in this case? Why?

2. How do the central issues relate to issues you've faced?

3. Why do you think Bill made his comment?

4. What assumptions do you think Bill has about June?

5. What are the other students in the class likely to be thinking? About Bill and June?

6. The faculty member has chosen to make an intervention. What should be the nature of the intervention? Why?

7. What institutional conditions might support addressing this situation in a productive manner? What conditions might hinder a supportive response?

8. What situations have you encountered that resemble this one? How did you respond? Given your experience, what would you do now?

Vignette #11: Trapped in Stereotypes

I. SYNOPSIS

Vern Edwards is your advisee and comes to you with a concern. Vern is a full member of the Navaho nation who grew up on his tribe's reservation. He shows you the comments from his professor on a paper he developed for a writing course. The professor rejected the paper on the grounds that Vern's style is too White and middle-class and does not reflect his tribal roots. Vern is visibly upset and pleads with you, "Do something and help me out."

II. TEACHING NOTES: TRAPPED IN STEREOTYPES

Introduction

The purpose of this teaching Vignette is to explore how stereotypes can limit a faculty member's assessment of student work. This Vignette shows how the faculty advisor is given an opportunity to address the specific instance and the more general issue associated with fairness in assessment.

An analysis of the strengths of stereotypes in accepting the diversity of human experience and the differences that can exist among members of an identified social group will generate discussion of the nature of diversity.

This Vignette can also be used to examine the responsibility of a faculty member to help educate a colleague in support of a student.

Discussion Questions

1. What is happening in this case? What surprised you in this case? Why?

2. How do the central issues relate to issues you've faced?

3. Why do you think the professor of writing made the comments to Vern?

4. What assumptions do you think the student had about that professor?

5. What do you think Vern is really asking for when he asks for help?

6. What should the faculty advisor do in this situation?

7. What institutional conditions might support addressing this situation in a productive manner? What conditions might hinder a supportive response?

8. What situations have you encountered that resemble this one? How did you respond? Given your experience, what would you do now?

Vignette #12: Why Learn a Second Language?

I. SYNOPSIS

Brian McCloud is a discussion leader in a first-year experience course in World Affairs. Normally, the discussions are lively and reinforce topics from the large lecture and in the readings. Today, the topic of the value of learning a second language took center stage. During the discussion, several students made it known that they spoke languages in addition to English, including Cantonese, French, and Spanish. Yvonne, one of the Spanish speakers, shared that her family speaks only Spanish because they immigrated to the U.S. relatively recently. Other students nodded and seem to be supportive of her willingness to share. As the discussion drew to a close, Amy, a bright and self-confident student asserted, "I agree, learning Spanish is something I should do. I have to be able to speak to our gardener." With time running out, the students looked down, closed their books, and suddenly the class-room was empty.

II. TEACHING NOTES: WHY LEARN A SECOND LANGUAGE?

Introduction

The purpose of this teaching Vignette is to consider the role of the faculty member in supporting students and managing hurtful state-ments. The Vignette shows how teachers need to be able to manage in the moment.

With this Vignette, an analysis of the role of socio-economic class and position in society can generate discussion about how to manage differences on this dimension in the classroom.

Discussion Questions

1. What is happening in this case? What surprised you in this case? Why?

2. How do the central issues relate to issues you've faced?

3. What impact does Amy's comment have on the discussion in the classroom?

4. What is the instructor's role in educating Amy?

5. What is the instructor's role in supporting Yvonne?

6. How likely is it that there is another student in the class who understands and has empathy for Yvonne's view and experience? For Amy's?

7. What should the faculty member do to support the rest of the class?

8. What institutional conditions might support addressing this situation in a productive manner? What conditions might hinder a supportive response?

9. What situations have you encountered that resemble this one? How did you respond? Given your experience, what would you do now?

Vignette #13: The Case of Quid Pro Quo

I. SYNOPSIS

Professor Smith is teaching an advanced undergraduate special topics seminar that meets from 6 PM to 8 PM two days a week. The course content is engaging and leads to lively discussions. Professor Smith is divorced and has dated graduate students in the past. After giving out an assignment at the close of class, he turns to two of the female students and says, "Girls, this is a challenging assignment. I can provide you assistance if you stop by my office after class tonight. You know, I do the grading."

Surprised by his comment, the two students glance at one another and hurriedly leave the classroom. Several other students observe the interaction uncomfortably and say nothing.

II. TEACHING NOTES: THE CASE OF QUID PRO QUO

Introduction

The purpose of this teaching Vignette is to demonstrate the role of power dynamics in the development of a potential sexual harassment scenario.

This Vignette provides an opportunity to examine and apply the legal guidelines for determining the occurrence of sexual harassment. In addition, a more general discussion of the nature of male–female interaction between faculty members and students can be used to explore factors that differentiate effective and ineffective teaching strategies.

Discussion Questions

1. What is happening in this case? What surprised you in this case? Why?
2. How do the central issues relate to issues you've faced?
3. What assumptions do you think Professor Smith is making about his students?
4. Is he really extending an offer of assistance? What do you think the students think?
5. What assumptions do you think the students have about Professor Smith?
6. What is the responsibility of the other students, especially the male students, in this situation? How can they be supported in doing the right thing (assuming there is one)?
7. What institutional conditions might support addressing this situation in a productive manner? What conditions might hinder a productive response?
8. What situations have you encountered that resemble this one? How did you respond? Given your experience, what would you do now?

Vignette #14: The Missing Interpreter

I. SYNOPSIS

Professor Delgado's Introduction to Physics course meets twice a week in a large lecture hall. She has high standards for herself and her students. This term, for the first time in her career, she has a hearing-impaired student, Julie, in her class. As per university practice, a paid interpreter attends the course and signs the lecture to the student who is in need of assistance. With a large class, Professor Delgado does not customarily learn her students' names, and she feels that doing so for this student would be seen as playing favorites and unfair to the other students in the class.

On Tuesday, as class is about to begin, Professor Delgado observes that the interpreter is nowhere to be seen. Not knowing sign language

and being concerned about losing time to cover the material planned
for the day, she begins the class as if the interpreter were present.

Julie, the student with the hearing impairment, realizes what is happening and sits through the class session in silence with tears streaming
down her face. The students sitting near Julie notice and appear
extremely uncomfortable. At the end of class, Professor Delgado
quickly leaves the room.

II. TEACHING NOTES: THE MISSING INTERPRETER

Introduction

The purpose of this teaching Vignette is to explore the role that
understanding and appreciating difference have in managing the learning environment. In this Vignette, the definition of fairness and equal
treatment and its impact on reasonable accommodation can be discussed in terms of the learning consequences.

The Vignette also allows for a discussion of the question of people's
comfort with others who are different, especially those with physical
challenges.

Discussion Questions

1. What is happening in this case? What surprised you in this case?
   Why?
2. How do the central issues relate to issues you've faced?
3. What assumptions do you think Professor Delgado has about her role
   as instructor?
4. What impact does her action have on the other students, especially
   those sitting near Julie?
5. How might have the interpreter have been able to help minimize
   the impact of his or her being absent? How might Julie have been
   able to participate in such a process?
6. What other forms of reasonable accommodation could Professor Delgado have provided that would not compromise her standards?
7. What institutional conditions might support addressing this situation
   in a productive manner?
8. To what extent is Professor Delgado legally liable for her actions?
9. What institutional conditions might support addressing this situation
   in a productive manner? What conditions might hinder a supportive
   response?

10. What situations have you encountered that resemble this one? How did you respond? Given your experience, what would you do now?

Vignette #15: The Professor Wants Particpation

I. SYNOPSIS

Professor John Bailey's approach to teaching Introduction to American Government is highly participatory. He strongly believes that student learning is maximized by active discussion and learning to thoughtfully argue one's position. He also believes that the course content is linked to the teaching approach because he feels that being able to critically evaluate and argue political issues is integral to being an informed citizen in a democracy.

This term, Professor Bailey has Than Nguyen as a student in his class. Than is an excellent student and has spent all of his life in the United States. His parents came to the United States as political refugees and have instilled in him a healthy respect for authority and saving face.

During the first few weeks of the term Professor Bailey notices that Than appears unwilling to speak up, especially in the confrontational settings of debate he has designed for the class. Feeling that he must do something to involve him, he confronts Than directly in class with questions about a current event in the national news and asks him to defend his viewpoint.

Than's response is to look at the floor and say, "Yes, Professor Bailey."

II. TEACHING NOTES: THE PROFESSOR WANTS PARTICIPATION

Introduction

The purpose of this teaching Vignette is to demonstrate that good intentions can lead to disappointing results if context is not taken into consideration.

This Vignette illustrates the fact that cultural styles, both the student's and the instructor's, impact effective teaching and learning and should be taken into account in curriculum design and delivery.

An analysis of how one can mesh course objectives with student learning and cultural styles can generate insight into addressing situations such as this.

Discussion Questions

1. What is happening in this case? What surprised you in this case? Why?
2. How do the central issues relate to issues you've faced?
3. What assumptions do you think Professor Bailey has about his role as instructor?
4. How can his approach to education in this course be best described?
5. How does it meet the learning styles of students such as Than?
6. What might Professor Bailey have done differently as he discovered that Than was withdrawing from the discussions in class?
7. What institutional conditions might support addressing this situation in a productive manner? What conditions might hinder a supportive response?
8. What situations have you encountered that resemble this one? How did you respond? Given your experience, what would you do now?

Vignette #16: The Higher Standard

I. SYNOPSIS

Anita Galvin would like to work with Professor Carmen Diaz, who is the only Latina faculty member in the department. Anita notices that Diaz has several male White students working in her lab and their grades are not as good as hers. She approaches Diaz during her office hours and asks what she needs to do to work in the lab because she is interested in gaining research experience so she can strengthen her portfolio for getting into graduate school.

Dr. Diaz responds to Anita by telling her that she needs to work harder than the other students because she is a Latina and that is just the way it is and that is what Diaz had to do to get where she is. In response, Anita says she is willing to work hard and feels her grades prove that she is already being successful.

Dr. Diaz says fine, and suggests Anita go work with one of the White faculty members in the department.

II. TEACHING NOTES: THE HIGHER STANDARD

Introduction

The purpose of this teaching Vignette is to explore the dilemma that surrounds embedded racism and the utilization of role models.

This Vignette begs a discussion of whether implicit racism and sexism is operating or if the reality of higher education requires talented minority students to have "independent" authorization to be recognized as legitimate.

Discussion Questions

1. What is happening in this case? What surprised you in this case? Why?

2. How do the central issues relate to issues you've faced?

3. How likely is it that Professor Diaz is trying to truly help Anita be successful by turning her away? If so, what factors would lead her to believe this to be the case?

4. What reasons, other than those stated, could be motivating Dr. Diaz to reject Anita's request?

5. How could Anita have been better able to convince Diaz (if at all)?

6. What institutional conditions might support addressing this situation in a productive manner? What conditions might hinder a supportive response?

7. What situations have you encountered that resemble this one? How did you respond? Given your experience, what would you do now?

Vignette #17: Are Learning Disabilites Real?

I. SYNOPSIS

On the first day of class Professor Montague Drew gives an overview of the course, and details the schedule of activities, assignments, and exams. As he explains the exam procedures he says, "For those of you who have what today we call learning disabilities, you will find that my class is very challenging. In my day, we did not have such conditions. Of course you will need to provide formal documentation in order to get special dispensation from me so you can obtain privileged treatment."

At this point several students look up and one of them says, "Are you serious?"

II. TEACHING NOTES: ARE LEARNING DISABILITIES REAL?

Introduction

The purpose of this teaching Vignette is to explore how fairness is defined and how that definition impacts effective learning.

This Vignette also demonstrates how the need to comply with legally prescribed accommodation can result in actions that follow the letter of the law but not the spirit of the law.

Discussion Questions

1. What is happening in this case? What surprised you in this case? Why?

2. How do the central issues relate to issues you've faced?

3. What assumptions do you think Professor Drew has about student learning and its assessment?

4. How do Professor Drew's statements set the climate for learning in the course?

5. What are the likely reactions by students in the class? Do you anticipate that a complaint might be filed or brought to the attention of another faculty member of the department chair? If so, what is likely to occur? If not why?

6. What institutional conditions might support addressing this situation in a productive manner? What conditions might hinder a supportive response?

7. What situations have you encountered that resemble this one? How did you respond? Given your experience, what would you do now?

Vignette #18: The Meaning of English

I. SYNOPSIS

On the first day of class, Professor Wade hands out the course syllabus. In a section entitled, "For International Students," the syllabus reads, "If English is your second language you will find this course to be very difficult. You will need to spend significantly more time than your native English-speaking peers on the readings, written assignments, and especially in preparing for oral presentations. Meeting the standards for English in this course is your responsibility and it is not your instructor's, as this is not a class in English as a second language."

Ali, a student from Egypt who graduated from secondary school in the United Kingdom, raises his hand and asks, "With all due respect Professor Wade, I just read the section in the syllabus for International Students. It does not offer advice for the situation where English is your third or fourth language." In response to his comment the class breaks out in laughter. Wade responds by saying, "You think your Queen's English is an advantage, don't you?"

II. TEACHING NOTES: THE MEANING OF ENGLISH

Introduction

The purpose of this teaching Vignette is to demonstrate the volatility associated with attitudes about English language competencies and the faculty–student power relationship.

A discussion of the association between language, nationality, and ethnicity can generate a full discussion of how language can be a surrogate for other forms of "difference."

This Vignette can also be analyzed in terms of the role expectations of faculty members who are asked to assist students without having the resources (e.g., training/expertise, time) to "adequately" meet the expectation.

Discussion Questions

1. What is happening in this case? What surprised you in this case? Why?

2. How do the central issues relate to issues you've faced?

3. What assumptions do you think Professor Wade is making about individuals for whom English is their second language?

4. How does Professor Wade view his role as an instructor?

5. What assumptions about language competencies does Ali have?

6. What does Ali's comment provoke in Professor Wade's response to him?

7. What institutional conditions might support addressing this situation in a productive manner? What conditions might hinder a supportive response?

8. What situations have you encountered that resemble this one? How did you respond? Given your experience, what would you do now?

Vignette #19: Mathematics and Ethnicity

I. SYNOPSIS

Professor Loomis is interested in helping students do well in his calculus class. After reviewing student performance at mid-term, he notices that David Lee, a Chinese-American student who is quite personable, is passing the course but nowhere near the top of the class. Loomis believes that something is wrong so he invites Lee to come to his office for an advising session.

When Lee arrives, Loomis greets him with, "David, thank you for stopping by. I am concerned with your performance in my class. You Asian students always do very well in my calculus class. You are only getting a B−. What is the difficulty?" In response, David, who is majoring in English literature and has never been strong in mathematics, finds himself speechless and looks at Professor Loomis with amazement.

II. TEACHING NOTES: MATHEMATICS AND ETHNICITY

Introduction

The purpose of this teaching Vignette is to demonstrate the power of stereotypes in misdirecting attributions and subverting strategies for enhancing student learning.

This Vignette can be used to discuss how individual members of identifiable groups vary from what is considered typical and how group-based categorizing is often an inaccurate basis for making judgments.

An analysis of the situation presented in this Vignette, when the group affiliation of the student was masked, would likely lead to a different set of outcomes.

Discussion Questions

1. What is happening in this case? What surprised you in this case? Why?
2. How do the central issues relate to issues you've faced?
3. What assumptions is Professor Loomis making about students of Asian descent? How does this impact his allocation of resources?
4. What impact is this likely to have on students, both of Asian descent and others?
5. What institutional conditions might support addressing this situation in a productive manner? What conditions might hinder a supportive response?
6. What situations have you encountered that resemble this one? How did you respond? Given your experience, what would you do now?

Vignette #20: So You Are Competent?

I. SYNOPSIS

Kareem Jones is meeting with his advisor midway through his second term on campus. Kareem is a student-athlete and is enjoying his time on campus thus far. The football team had a good season and even as a first-year player he was able to get in some playing time. He is enjoying his academic experience as well, completing his first term with an A in Calculus, a B− in English Composition, and an A− in Introductory Psychology.

Professor Robbins, his advisor, asks Kareem about his experience at the university, and Kareem describes his achievements and his interest in exploring the sciences as his next goal. Robbins responds by saying, "This is impressive. Kareem, you beat all the statistical predictions for a person like you. I think you ought to take a lighter load next term. You don't want to tempt fate. You are still a first-year student and if your grades drop now, that will hurt your academic standing significantly. You should take the hard courses after you get further into your studies. You should take more basic, skill-building courses now so you can guarantee you will do well in the future."

Kareem, as a first-year student, respects Professor Robbins' experience and expertise. After all, Robbins is a professor. However, he is troubled by the advice. "Why should I take those 'gut' courses," he thinks to himself. "I did well in classes that other students had difficulty with. Something does not make sense."

II. TEACHING NOTES: SO YOU ARE COMPETENT?

Introduction

The purpose of this teaching Vignette is to demonstrate how stereotypes can marginalize the student and lead to discounting the student's talents. In the service of "protecting" students, we can reduce student motivation and create self-doubt as opposed to self-confidence.

This Vignette can be used to open a discussion of what the role of an advisor is in empowering students to be successful and how difference impacts this objective.

Discussion Questions

1. What is happening in this case? What surprised you in this case? Why?
2. How do the central issues relate to issues you've faced?
3. What assumptions do you think Professor Robbins has about minority student-athletes?
4. What impact is Professor Robbins likely to have on students like Kareem?
5. In this situation, what courses will Kareem sign up for? How will this likely impact his broader academic career?
6. What institutional conditions might support addressing this situation in a productive manner? What conditions might hinder a supportive response?
7. What situations have you encountered that resemble this one? How did you respond? Given your experience, what would you do now?

Vignette # 21: Is He Racist?

I. SYNOPSIS

Dr. Gerry Byrne teaches a course in American history covering the period of time before 1880. To understand the role of African American soldiers during the Civil War, the class views the film, *Glory*. During the discussion and debriefing after the film, Dr. Byrne announces to the class: "I showed you this film to illustrate the critical role colored soldiers played in the Civil War." The next day, two African American students in the class complain to the chair of the history department that the faculty member's use of the term "colored" is racist.

II. TEACHING NOTES: IS HE RACIST?

Introduction

The purpose of this teaching Vignette is to consider the role of the faculty member in designing learning experiences for college students. The Vignette illustrates the challenge of using appropriate language to describe historically marginalized groups.

The Vignette is designed to focus on issues of student support, but can also be used to discuss faculty members' ability to engage students in discussions of historical topics.

Discussion Questions

1. What is happening in this case? What surprised you in this case? Why?

2. How do the central issues relate to issues you've faced?

3. Why do you think the faculty member showed the film and guided a follow-up discussion in a college history course? What are the pros and cons of these decisions?

4. What role should the faculty member play in supporting the students who spoke out in this situation?

5. How would you recommend the department chair handle this situation? (i.e., what should she say and do?)

6. To what extent do you think the faculty member should take responsibility for exploring the concerns of the students who brought the issue to the attention of the department chair?

7. What institutional conditions might support addressing this situation in a productive manner? What conditions might hinder a supportive response?

8. What situations have you encountered that resemble this one? How did you respond? Given your experience, what would you do now?

Vignette #22: The "Suspicious" Character

I. SYNOPSIS

Mark Nolan, a faculty member at a private university in the Midwest, gazes out his office window contemplating the devastating events of September 11, 2001. As he ponders his upcoming meeting with students in his political science course, he notices a bearded man lingering in the parking lot below. The man is studying a manual of some sort as students move hurriedly between classes. Dr. Nolan continues observing the dark-skinned man until most of the students have made their way to class and the area is quiet. Suddenly the man looks up and locks eyes with him in surprise, realizing he is being observed. He hurries off and enters a building across the square from Dr. Nolan's observation post. Dr. Nolan moves quickly to the phone, calls campus security to report this man's behavior, and walks quickly to class.

Twenty minutes later, there is a knock on Dr. Nolan's classroom door. He excuses himself in front of the class and walks toward the door. Astonished, he finds the bearded man accompanied by a campus security officer. The bearded man smiles warmly, extends his hand, and takes a seat in the front row of the class. The security officer mentions to Dr. Nolan that the man is a registered student in his class.

II. TEACHING NOTES: THE "SUSPICIOUS" CHARACTER

Introduction

The purpose of this Vignette is to consider the role of the faculty member in supporting students. The case shows how both teachers and staff members struggle to balance personal freedoms with respectful treatment of others.

The Vignette is designed to focus on issues of student support, but can also be used to discuss issues of faculty–student communication, student–student communication, and faculty members' involvement in life outside of the classroom.

An analysis using principles of prejudice reduction and student support is especially applicable to this teaching case.

Discussion Questions

1. What is happening in this case? What surprised you? Why?
2. How would you describe the critical issues in the case?
3. What was your first reaction to this situation? Why did you have this reaction?

4. What assumptions did you make about Mark, the security officer, and the student?

5. What actions might Mark take? What are the consequences of these actions for Mark and the student?

6. What course of action would you take if you were Mark? Why?

7. If you had to recommend how to handle this situation to another faculty member, what would you say?

8. What institutional conditions might support addressing this situation in a productive manner? What conditions might hinder a supportive response?

9. What situations have you encountered that resemble this one? How did you respond? Given your experience, what would you do now?

Vignette #23: The Case of Mistaken Identity

I. SYNOPSIS

Professor Willis sits in his office expecting a package from central administration with the applications from the candidates for the Director of Human Resources search. He is a key member of the search committee and is responsible for reviewing the applications and candidate qualifications. While waiting, he is grading students' papers from the last assignment.

Ignacio Rivera is a work-study student who works in the office of the Vice President for Business Affairs. Ignacio is five feet six inches tall and has dark skin. He is also an honor student in chemistry and has been preparing for the Medical School Admissions Exam.

As part of his duties, Ignacio is delivering the candidates' materials to Professor Willis. He stops by Willis's office and knocks at the open door. Willis looks up at him and says, "Oh yes, you can empty the garbage can over there. Thank you."

Ignacio, being taken aback and confused, steps back and excuses himself, leaving the package in the department office.

Later, Willis wonders why the package was left in his mailbox.

II. TEACHING NOTES: THE CASE OF MISTAKEN IDENTITY

Introduction

The purpose of this Vignette is to illustrate how appearances are associated with stereotypes that marginalize others. In this Vignette, the student is mistaken for a custodian on the basis of observable characteristics that are associated with stereotypes.

An analysis of the disservice of stereotypes, for this student and those who work in lower-status occupations, will generate fruitful discussion.

Discussion Questions

1. What is happening in this case? What surprised you in this case? Why?
2. How do the central issues relate to issues you've faced?
3. What assumptions do you think Professor Willis has about custodians?
4. What assumptions do you think Professor Willis has about honor students?
5. Ignacio reacted by leaving the office and dropping off the package in the department office. What are some other ways might he have reacted? What would have been the consequences of reacting in other ways in comparison to the way described in the Vignette?
6. What would you do if Ignacio told you about this experience?
7. What institutional conditions might support addressing this situation in a productive manner? What conditions might hinder a supportive response?
8. What situations have you encountered that resemble this one? How did you respond? Given your experience, what would you do now?

Vignette #24: Derailed by a Stereotype

I. SYNOPSIS

Chantelle Green is a sophomore taking a statistics class required for entry into her chosen field. This is her first class in statistics, and she is finding it both challenging and interesting. She did well on her first exam, scoring a high B+. This past week the instructor introduced the topic of dispersion and the concept of the standard deviation. Because Chantelle is interested in the concept and doing well in the course she arranges a session with the instructor.

When she arrives at the meeting she introduces herself and asks the instructor for advice on one of the supplemental problems at the end of the chapter. In response, the instructor says, "I am glad you dropped by. You know that people like you typically have problems with statistics. I understand it is a cultural problem, so don't feel bad about it. Let me work problem 7 out with you here. OK...."

Chantelle, listens to the instructor talk through problem 7 and then politely leaves, discouraged and feeling the faculty member just was not there.

II. TEACHING NOTES: DERAILED BY A STEREOTYPE

Introduction

The purpose of this Vignette is to demonstrate how stereotypes can marginalize the student and lead to offering help in a manner that discounts the student's talents.

In this Vignette, a successful student is not listened to by an instructor who, in attempting to be of assistance, communicates a lack of confidence in the student's ability.

An analysis of the process of genuine helping and mentoring in the context of this Vignette can remind us of how minority students are often sent messages that they are not able to succeed.

Discussion Questions

1. What is happening in this case? What surprised you in this case? Why?

2. How do the central issues relate to issues you've faced?

3. What assumptions do you think Chantelle's statistics professor has about minority females?

4. What impact is this professor likely to have on students like Chantelle?

5. What else could Chantelle have done in response to the professor's response to her question?

6. What institutional conditions might support addressing this situation in a productive manner? What conditions might hinder a supportive response?

7. What situations have you encountered that resemble this one? How did you respond? Given your experience, what would you do now?

INDEX

About the Author

JOSEPH E. GARCIA is Associate Dean and Director of the Center for Excellence in Management Education at Western Washington University, Bellingham, WA. He has published several textbooks on managerial skills and a research monograph on leadership.

KAREN J. HOELSCHER is Professor of Elementary Education in the Woodring College of Education at Western Washington University, Bellingham, WA. In 2001, Hoelscher received Western Washington University's Diversity Achievement Award.